ENCYCLOPAEDIA OF EMINENT THINKERS

VOLUME-XXIX **MAULANA ABUL KALAM AZAD**

Volumes by the same author

The Political Thought of ***Veer Savarkar***
The Political Thought of ***M.A. Jinnah***
The Political Thought of ***Mohammad Iqbal***
The Political Thought of ***K.B. Hedgewar***
The Political Thought of ***M.S. Golwalkar***
The Political Thought of ***Lokmanya Bal Gangadhar Tilak***
The Political Thought of ***Pandit Deendayal Upadhyaya***
The Political Thought of ***Gopal Krishna Gokhale***
The Political Thought of ***Maulana Abul Kalam Azad***
The Political Thought of ***Sir Syed Ahmed Khan***

About the Author

Dr. Jai Narain Sharma (*b.* 1951) is Professor and Chairman of the Department of Gandhian Studies, Panjab University, Chandigarh. He is also Hon. Director of Gandhi Bhawan; member of Board of Studies, Nagpur University, Nagpur and Mahatma Gandhi Kashi Vidyapith, Varanasi; member of Research Degree Committee of the Department of Political Science, H.P. University, Shimla: General Secretary of Indian Soviety of Gandhian Studies; and member on the Presidium of the Alliance for Sarvodaya. He regularly writes for leading newspapers, and has published more than hundred research papers in professional journals of repute. Dr. Sharma has many books to his credit including *"Gandhi's View of Political Power"*, *"Economics of Defence: A Study of SAARC Countries"*, *"Economic Thought of Mahatma Gandhi"*, *"Human Resource Management"*, *"Alternative Economics: Economics of Mahatma Gandhi and Globalisation"*, *"Power, Politics and Corruption: A Gandhian Solution"* and *"Research Methodology: The Discipline and its Dimensions.*

ENCYCLOPAEDIA OF EMINENT THINKERS

VOLUME-XXIX

THE POLITICAL THOUGHT OF MAULANA ABUL KALAM AZAD

Jai Narain Sharma
Professor & Chairman
Department of Gandhian Studies
Panjab University,
Chandigarh

CONCEPT PUBLISHING COMPANY, NEW DELHI-110 059

ISBN 13-978-81-7022-684-0 (Series) ISBN 10-81-7022-684-8 (Series)
ISBN 13-978-81-8069-637-4 (Vol. XXIX) ISBN 10-81-8069-637-5 (Vol. XXIX)

First Published 2010

Published and Printed by

Concept
Since 1974

Concept Publishing Company

Regd. Office:

A/15-16, Commercial Block, Mohan Garden
New Delhi-110059 (India)
Phones : 25351460, 25351794, *Fax* : 091-11-25357109
Email : publishing@conceptpub.com,
Website: www.conceptpub.com

Editorial Office:

H-13, Bali Nagar, New Delhi-110 015, India.

Cataloging in Publication Data-- *Courtesy:* D.K. Agencies (P) Ltd. docinfo@dkagencies.com

Encyclopaedia of eminent thinkers.
v. 26-30 cm. -- (Gandhian studies and peace research series ; 11)
Vols. 11- lack series statement.
In Indian context.
Includes bibliographical references. Includes indexes.
Contents: v. 26. The political thought of C.R. Das / Ashu Pasricha -- v. 27 The political thought of Gopal Krishna Gokhale / Jai Narain Sharma -- v. 28. The political thought of Lala Lajpat Rai / Ashu Pasricha -- v. 29. The political thought of Maulana Abul Kalam Azad / Jai Narain Sharma - v. 30. The political thought of Sir Pherozeshah Mehta / Ashu Pasricha.
ISBN 13: 9788170226840 (set) ISBN 10: 8170226848 (set)

1. Statesmen--India. 2. Political science--India. 3. India--Politics and government. I. Sharma, Jai Narain, 1951- II. Pasricha, Ashu, 1967- III. Series: Gandhian studies and peace research series ; 11.

DDC 954.035 22

DEDICATED
TO
THE SACRED MEMORY
OF
KHAJAN SINGH (BARSAN)
(My Dear Friend)

PREFACE

Maulana Abul Kalam Azad occupies a distinctive position in the history of our Freedom Movement. An erudite person, Maulana Azad was one of the few Philosopher-Statesmen our nation has been gifted with. Emotionally and intellectually he was very close to both Mahatma Gandhi and Jawaharlal Nehru. During the Freedom Movement and in the years immediately following independence, he was closely associated with crucial decision making in the country.

Maulana Azad was a man with a mission. His greatest mission in life, perhaps, was Hindu-Muslim unity and the unity and integrity of the country. He detested partition of the country. Once it became a reality, he wanted to minimise its damage for both the sides by encouraging linkages at various levels between the two countries.

Maulana Azad was a many-splendoured, multi-faceted personality. He was at once a great scholar, a distinguished writer, a powerful orator, an ardent patriot, a zealous freedom fighter and a great leader with tenacious determination, a rare sagacity and vision. His mission was for national integration and unity of the country. It is a paradox of history that a great scholar born and brought up in a Muslim family, soaked in Islamic principles and steeped in deeply religious and mystical pursuits becomes an impassioned advocate for nationalism while Mohammad Ali Jinnah with thoroughly Western education and outlook should align himself with conservative and obscurantist elements and espouse the cause of separatism. Maulana Azad was a strange combination of scholastic rationalism and also a modern outlook. Through his writings in his famous journals—*Al-Hilal* and *Al-Balagh*, and through his moving speeches he caused a sensation in Muslim intellectual circles and created a ferment in the minds of the younger generation. He wanted to rouse the people of his own community to join the national mainstream and fight unitedly with his brethren for the freedom of the country. This is one of his great contributions. In fact, there are two contributions of Maulana which are outstanding. One is, his contribution in the field of practical politics and that is to bring the Muslim to join the freedom movement. That is a great achievement which history has inscribed in golden letters and the other is his theory or doctrine of unity of all religions.

His prodigious knowledge, pursuit of excellence in life, sharp and luminous intellect, steadfastness of purpose, his view of life, politics, religion, public morality and incisive world-view will continue to inspire the generations to come.

My work has benefited from the advice and suggestions of Professor R.N. Pal, former Pro-Vice Chancellor Panjab University Patiala, Dr. K.S. Bharti, Head Department of Gandhian Thought Nagpur University Nagpur, Dr. A.D. Mishra, Deputy Director, National Gandhi Museum, New Delhi, Dr. R.P Duvedi, Head, Department of Gandhian Thought, Mahatma Gandhi Kashi Vidyapith, Varanasi, Professor B.R. Duggar,s Jain Vishwabharati Institute, Deemed University, Ladnun, Professor Raj Singh, Department of Sociology, H.A.U. Hissar, Professor Rakesh Dutta and Dr. (Ms) Meena Dutta, Department of Defence and Strategic Analysis, Panjab University, Chandigarh.

I am deeply indebted to my colleagues in the department Dr. M.L. Sharma and Dr. Ashu Pasricha who were good enough to read through a draft of the book and from whose many penetrating criticism and constructive suggestions I have benefited more than I can say.

There are many other teacher colleagues and students who have contributed in so many ways and I express my thanks to them.

To my wife Rashmi, I owe the deepest debt of all for her emotional support, her unfailing encouragement and her undispensable contribution towards providing the environment in which I could complete this work.

Thanks are also due to my publisher Shri Ashok Kumar Mittal for the keen interest he has shown in this project.

Chandigarh **JAI NARAIN SHARMA**

CONTENTS

Encyclopaedia of Eminent Thinkers Series

Vol. I. The Political Thought of Mahatma Gandhi/ *K.S. Bharti*
Vol. II. The Political Thought of Nehru/ *K.S. Bharti*
Vol. III. The Political Thought of Rabindra Nath Tagore/ *K.S. Bharti*
Vol. IV. The Political Thought of Radhakrishnan/ *K.S. Bharti*
Vol. V. The Political Thought of Vinoba/ *K.S. Bharti*
Vol. VI. The Political Thought of Aurobindo/ *K.S. Bharti*
Vol. VII. The Political Thought of Jayaprakash Narayan/ *K.S. Bharti*
Vol. VIII. The Political Thought of Vivekananda/ *K.S. Bharti*
Vol. IX. The Political Thought of Ambedkar/ *K.S. Bharti*
Vol. X. The Political Thought of M.N. Roy/ *K.S. Bharti*
Vol. XI. The Political Thought of Dadabhai Naoroji/ *Ashu Pasricha*
Vol. XII. The Political Thought of Veer Savarkar/ *Jai Narain Sharma*
Vol. XIII. The Political Thought of M.A. Jinnah/ *Jai Narain Sharma*
Vol. XIV. The Political Thought of Tej Bahadur Sapru/ *Ashu Pasricha*
Vol. XV. The Political Thought of C. Rajagopalachari/ *Ashu Pasricha*
Vol. XVI. The Political Thought of Subhas Chandra Bose/ *Ashu Pasricha*
Vol. XVII. The Political Thought of Mohammad Iqbal/ *Jai Narain Sharma*
Vol. XVIII. The Political Thought of K.B. Hedgewar/ *Jai Narain Sharma*
Vol. XIX. The Political Thought of Bhagat Singh/ *Ashu Pasricha*
Vol. XX. The Political Thought of M.S. Golwalkar/ *Jai Narain Sharma*
Vol. XXI. The Political Thought of Sir Syed Ahmed Khan/ *Jai Narain Sharma*
Vol. XXII. The Political Thought of Mahadev Govind Ranade/ *Ashu Pasricha*
Vol. XXIII. The Political Thought of Pandit Deendayal Upadhyaya/ *Jai Narain Sharma*
Vol. XXIV. The Political Thought of Lokmanya Bal Gangadhar Tilak/ *Jai Narain Sharma*
Vol. XXV. The Political Thought of Annie Besant/ *Ashu Pasricha*
Vol. XXVI. The Political Thought of C.R. Das/ *Ashu Pasricha*
Vol. XXVII. The Political Thought of Gopal Krishna Gokhale/ *Jai Narain Sharma*
Vol. XXVIII. The Political Thought of Lala Lajpat Rai/ *Ashu Pasricha*
Vol. XXIX. The Political Thought of Maulana Abul Kalam Azad/ *Jai Narain Sharma*
Vol. XXX. The Political Thought of Sir Pherozeshah Mehta/ *Ashu Pasricha*

1

LIFE AND ACTIVITIES

Mohiuddin Ahmad, who later come to be known as Maulana Abul Kalám Azad, was the scion of a family of *peers* (eminent religious preceptors). His ancestors had served the Mughals but, unreconciled to the atmosphere generated by the ascendancy of the British power, had shifted to Mecca some time before 1857. His father Khairuddin married an Arab woman and therefore Arabic language become,Mohiuddin's mother tongue. Their residence was close to the grand mosque in Mecca and the young boy heard the call to prayer being recited in mellifluous tones, which must have created in him a sense of respect for the religion of Islam as well as love of music. The family atmosphere was deeply suffused with religiosity, his father being an eminent *peer* commanding a large following of disciples.

Mohiuddin was very young, about six or seven years of age, when his father shifted the family to India, first to Bombay and then to Calcutta. Shortly after arrival in Calcutta his mother died and the father wished again to go back to Mecca but his disciples persuaded him to change his mind so Calcutta became the permanent home of the family, though it was from Delhi that they had shifted to Mecca.

His education had started in Mecca itself where he was taught by specially engaged teachers at home. His father probably did not like his son to be spoilt by the outside influence,hence he was not sent to any school but taught at home, privately. His secluded life insulted in two tendencies: love of books, they being the only companions, and the curiosity about the world beyond the four walls of the house. The visitors at their home were, by and large, the disciples of his father who treated young Mohiuddin, the son of their peer, with the same reverence that they displayed towards his father. It was rather irksome for the young lad, who wanted companions to share his thoughts. Thus grew in him an aversion to the system of religious instructions followed by his father and other ulama. However, he showed extraordinary capacity to learn so that within three-four years he had mastered most of the syllabus prescribed for his study and was able to match his teachers in knowledge and argument.

Khairuddin was totally unaffected by any contemporary movement for reform, and totally opposed to English education. However would not also entrust his sons to the Calcutta madrasa, a theological school founded under British auspices. He taught them himself or called in scholars, eminent in their particular subject, provided they met with his approval. Azad says it was as if he thought the slightest breath of outside breeze would corrupt them. For a period of some months, Azad recalls being allowed to study medicine from well known Shias. But no one would have been allowed to come near him about whom his father had the slightest suspicion of 'Wahhabi' leanings. Early each morning, the boys studied with their father, and then the outside teachers came. The afternoons were devoted to study and memorization, and in the evenings their father tested them on the outside lessons or talked to them about some worthy topic. After evening prayers, he would give them another lesson.[1]

The syllabus for this education was the dars-e-Nizami, the curriculum of Islamic religious education prevalent in India since the eighteenth century, and for which Azad later expressed near contempt. Mentioning one aspect after another of the course, he repeats the verdict: 'worthless ... worthless' *(naqis)*. He says that consists solely of the old categories of *ulum-e-diniya* (religious sciences): *manqulat* (revealed sciences: chiefly Quranic *tafsir*, *hadith*, and *fiqh*), and *ma'qulat* (rational sciences: grammar, logic, philosophy, and mathematics). Of the former, he says that while one learns the content and meaning of the texts, such knowledge gives no 'insight tending to mental initiative'. As for the second category, he says that apart from logic, 'the rational sciences' are only a matter of memorization of one period of ancient philosophy, even though knowledge has advanced far beyond that. The method of learning mathematics bears no comparison to modern mathematics, and even that is not a required subject.[2]

Azad says that his father's method of teaching every subject was to start with the memorization of some text, because 'that was the method of teaching in the family of Shah Wallullah'.[3] He did go somewhat beyond the requirements of the dars-e-Nizami. For example, he was not satisfied with the few prescribed parts of Baidawi but taught the whole of it. He put great emphasis on logic and even included some outside subjects: medicine, mathematics, astronomy, and fortune-telling. He also taught some sufi texts of Ibn Arabi and Suhrawardi. But the major emphasis remained on *hadith, tafsir*, and *fiqh*, with the stress throughout on memorization. Many have testified that Azad had a phenomenal memory. Azad described the working of his own mind in 1922:

"I...have made compartments in my brain, hundreds and thousands of compartments. This compartment for law, this for international politics, this for history, this for mathematics, this for military science. I accumulate information in an orderly and systematic fashion, like a discriminating, accomplished store-keeper, in separate compartments. Whenever information is required at any particular time, I open the appropriate compartment and keep the other compartments closed...It is not a case of one compartment of the mind...At one and the same I have to open many compartments."[4]

This strong emphasis on rote memory is characteristic of Muslim traditional education, and continues to be so to this day. Azad's description unwittingly reveals the weakness of this training. He was able to accumulate fantastic stores of facts, but as significant as the number of compartments he could open at one time was his ability to keep others closed. His training, actually militated against the integration of his knowledge, the relation of knowledge in one area to knowledge in another. To some extent, of course, Azad's intelligence enabled him to overcome this effect of his early training. His later criticism of the dars-e-Nizami for failing to give insight tending to initiative is significant in this regard.

Azad learned his lessons quickly and well and from childhood found within himself a strong urge to talk about what he knew. So much a preacher was he that, when there was no one else to converse with, he would start a long speech before anyone who happened to be in the house. There was no shortage of disciples, few of whom were learned, the majority being common people. But whether educated or illiterate, considering him a *pirzada* (son of a pir), they applauded his every word and listened with the rapt attention of devotees. For the young boy this audience was a proving ground. Regularly after every evening worship, fifty to sixty people would sit outside the audience room and, whenever Azad sat there, they would ask him questions. This gave him the opportunity to display his virtuosity. He says he would lecture for hours and find intense pleasure therein. He was then no more than ten or eleven and became known in Calcutta as something of a boy wonder who preached sermons. His own comment was that what people meant by 'sermons' was just youthful 'nonsense' that he chattered before this group.[5]

A constant theme in the father's teaching and in all his conversation and preaching, which was to prove a big issue in the boy's thought, was his bitter opposition to the 'Wahhabi' position. What he objected to in the Waliullahis was not their emphasis on *jihad*, but their challenge to taqlid and their criticism of sufi beliefs and practices which they stigmatized as un-Islamic accretions. Such practices were, however, the very life of pirs like Khairuddin and their disciples. It was particularly galling that the 'Wahhabi' leader, Shah Ismail Shahid, should be a man from the family of Shah Waliullah, who was also a respected sufi. Azad heard Shah Ismail's name, as well as that of Sayyid Ahmad of Rai Bareilly, frequently. A stock joke of his father was to call Shah Ismail's famous book, 'Taghwiyat al-Iman' instead of *Taqwiyat al-Iman* ('Taking away the Faith' instead of *Strengthening the Faith).*[6]

From early childhood, Azad could remember hearing the terrible word 'Wahhabi'. He felt it referred to some sort of repulsive and hateful monster. The term was used in the home for rats and mosquitoes, and for an unfortunate disfigured fellow they sometimes saw outside the house. On one occasion, in his father's audience room, Azad was surprised to see an elderly bearded man with a turban, sitting respectfully, but with his father and everyone else so furious at him that the poor man was trembling. He innocently asked who the man was. 'A Wahhabi' was the stern reply. The boy was puzzled. This man did not have a discoloured face or a crooked mouth; there was nothing abnormal about his eyes, nor was his appearance in anyway hideous. He did not conform at all to the mental picture the child had of what a 'Wahhabi,' looked like. When he was older, Azad realized that in his sermons his father had constantly spoken against the 'Wahhabis'. Hundreds of times he heard him say that their *kufr* (unbelief) was worse than the kufr of Jews and Christians. 'The Jews and Christians do not deny their leaders, but these wicked people deny their Prophet.' Eventually Azad found out the facts for himself—that they did not deny the basic tenets of Islam or the Prophet himself—and felt sympathy for them which grew until ultimately he regarded himself as close to them. By that time, he had been investigating this '*wahhabiyat*' for himself and had begun to form his own opinion. He used to argue with his teachers, but he received no intellectual help from their method of discussion. He says they simply went round in accretions, bound to the old type of reasoning.

Azad's formal education, therefore, consisted of the dars-e-Nizami with slight modifications, all administered under the eagle eye if his father, with his rigid authoritarian views. This course of instruction, which would normally last until the age of twenty, Azad finished when he was fifteen and, as was the custom, was given a circle of students of his own to teach. Several years before this, stirrings of doubt began within him, which were eventually to lead him to claim that he had freed himself completely from the traditional religion of his father and had found his own faith. In fact, however, he rejected only certain aspects of his father's teaching. He remained, essentially, a product of his Muslim environment. Islam as expressed in Azad's life was very different in some respects from Islam as expressed in Khairuddin's life. But Azad continued to share much with his father. Variations within cultural groups may be very significant to those within, whereas to those outside the differences seem much less significant than the features they hold in common. Inhuman religious life particularly, it is a well-known phenomenon that the bitterest opposition can be between people who, in fact, agree on everything except the particular doctrinal points at issue. Azad thus came to regard himself as opposed to his father's version of Islam, whereas to others removed from the conflict between them he did not appear so very different. As Azad matured, he became less and less the type of Muslim represented by his father, but he never completely lost the characteristics of his orthodox upbringing. The importance of his early Islamic training must never be forgotten.

A Wider World

How does one, brought up in such an environment, escape into free inquiry? Azad claimed not to understand that 'power' that helped 'break the claims of family customs and traditions.' As a boy, he led a sheltered and secure life. In his words: 'surrounded by the four walls of taqlid and veneration of the past...no winds of change had any chance of passing within...as if I were living the life of a hundred years before.'[7] But his life was not completely devoid of outside influences. Whenever, ordinary people came to his house, or he encountered them in the street; he envied them and longed to be free like them. He was especially introduced to a wider world through his reading. His father regarded Arabic and Persian as the only permissible scholarly languages. Azad, however, liked to read Urdu books and developed a love for poetry. From the age of ten, Azad had to indulge his serious taste for Urdu literature surreptitiously. He spent a lot of money on books, kept them under his mattress, and read them by candlelight, often until one or two o'clock in the morning. Stealing time from sleep was the only way he could read what he really liked. His father suspected that he was looking at books other than the prescribed texts, strictly forbade it, and placed him under tighter surveillance. It was not surprising that the habits affected Azad's health. He never had time for any other recreation as all his 'energies were devoted to study'.[8]

Maulvi Abdul Wahid Khan helped develop Azad's taste for

Urdu and Persian poetry, suggested his *takhallus* (pen name), and helped him bring out his first paper, *Nairang-e-'Alam,* in which he published his poetic efforts. Although he later regarded his pen name, 'Azad' (free), as indicating his freedom from inherited beliefs, it was actually chosen for a more mundane reason. In his own words, 'the most important reason...was that in anthologies, poems were listed alphabetically by *takhallus*, and those beginning with *alif* ('a') would be first.' Azad's poetry, the work of his immature years, is not very important in itself, save that it reflects the initial efforts of a great literary stylist. Further, it enabled him to come into contact with important personalities and movements that helped enlarge his outlook and allowed him ultimately to break from the traditionalism of his surroundings.[9]

In 1899, when he was only eleven, he published the first issue of *Nairang-e-Alam*, hoping for a thousand subscribers. Only about 150 took it, and few of them paid their subscriptions in advance. 'But he did not lose heart and continued publication for several months. He recalled thinking as a boy that the highest human attainment would be the position of editor of a paper. A press owner persuaded him to publish one, and so, in 1900, at the age twelve, he brought out a weekly newspaper, *Misbah*, which ran for about three months. It had sections devoted to theological, historical and biographical topics, articles on such subjects as Man (faith), al-Ghazali, 'Newton and the Law of Gravity', and one on the 'Id festival, which he says was reprinted by other Urdu papers."[10]

He and his brother sent poetry and prose contributions too *Khadang-e-Nazr* of Lucknow, and its editor agreed to an increased prose section if Azad agneed to edit it. It was on the basis of an article on X-rays that Azad wrote for this paper that Shibli began to correspond with the young writer. Azad also wrote for *Makhzan*, one of the leading Urdu literary magazines of the day, and for *Tuhfa-e-Ahmadiya* and *Ahsan al-Akhbar*. These last two papers were both published in Calcutta , and edited by Maulvi Ahmad Husain Fatehpuri, who had a reputation for controversy with Christians. Azad praised him as a hard-working and able man and was indebted to him for his kindness.

In working for these papers, Azad not only earned some money and gained invaluable writing experience, but also first encountered newspapers from the Arab world. The office of Ahsan al-Akhbar in Calcutta subscribed to Egyptian and other Arab newspapers, and there he read the Cairo periodicals *al-Hilal, al-Muqtataf*, and *Rashid Rida's al-Manar*. This first hand acquaintance with Arabic writings developed the interest in the Arab world he already had because of his family background and childhood. Among other things, he read Abduh's refutation of Farah Antun (later published as Islam and Christianity) in *al-Manar*, and later recalled how this had enlivened his interest in religious discussion. His desire for new Arabic books developed from then on, and he spent as much as twenty to twenty-five rupees per month on book orders.[11]

The interest in religious discussion led to an increased interest in community activities. The annual meetings of the Nadwat ul-Ulama attracted him, but his disgust at the conduct of the opposing factions added to his revulsion against the orthodox ulama. These conferences actually stimulated his first attempts at polemical writing, in the form of answers to the tracts of the anti-Nadwa group.

A few years following his first diversification of interests, Azad also began to study in music. This too occurred because of his interest in books. Sometime in 1905, he happened to be thumbing through a Persian book in a Calcutta book-stall, when European principal of the Calcutta madrasa, a Persian scholar, asked the young man if he understood what he was reading. Azad replied indignantly that books were for understanding, but when challenged to read out a passage, had to admit that he did not understand what he read. This was a new experience for him. The subject of the book was music. So, not to be outdone, he got one of his father's disciples to teach him surreptitiously. He says he practised the sitar for four or five years, and that music became the one thing in life he could not live without.

His love of public speaking began very early too. In addition to the youthful 'nonsense' that he chattered before his father's disciples, his first experience was at the meetings of a society in Calcutta formed to encourage young men in writing and speaking. He confessed that, as a young man, he liked to defeat his opponents in public debate, and no meeting with a friend ever ended without an argument. Such arguments, though friendly, did not encourage give-and-take. Open discussion, in which his own ideas could develop through the contribution of his peers, have no place in this description of his early enthusiasms:

"Pleasure in these activities captivated me...I had to write articles. I had to publish a paper. I had to be an editor. I had to have a monthly journal. I had to make speeches, and the crowning success of speeches is to have a society—not just any society, but one with a specific object. These were the things that intoxicated me at that time."[12]

He had to hold forth, in other words. He did set up a society, complete with weekly meetings and a reading room. In this connection, Azad also admitted his debt to heredity. He claimed to have inherited his father's 'celebrated preaching ability', and said that his mother was also a fluent speaker. During the month of Ramazan, she used to speak to the women of good Meccan families who came to the house.

All these early activities then, were evidence of exposure to far wider interests than his father's training alone provided. Though he says he could recall every detail of that period, Azad still maintained that he could not understand what had caused him to revolt against the form of religion in which he had been brought up. He was well aware of his unusual endowment. Everything around him conspired to impress upon him the fact that he was special. What he did not realize was that in such a situation, where a boy of intelligence and individuality was faced with a dominant father figure, rebellion in some form was almost inevitable. Nevertheless, Azad's own account is revealing:

"My earliest recollection is of the aura of dignity and sanctity all around me, and I found my family honoured and reverenced as if they were idols. While I was still a child, thousands of men used to come and kiss my hands and feet as the son of a pir. Apart from my family elders, any man I ever saw was bowing before me, overawed with respect and homage. Extremely able and elderly men used to come and...sit with respect and homage just as if I were in fact their idol. To every word that escaped my lips, no matter how worthless and meaningless, they listened with bowed heads and very great confidence and respect, and to everything they responded with, 'Hear! Hear!' and 'Yes, indeed!'[13]

Azad said that usually the sons of pirs spend their time in this way and do not bother to study, but simply remain ignorant. Thanks to the tradition of learning in his family, his father's efforts, and his own interest, he escaped this fate. Still, he emphasised, the family atmosphere was extremely conservative; his father had no time for the question 'why?' and directed two-third of his writings against Muslims of the school which challenged these practices. All his teachers and all his books were like this. So, as he saw it, there was no reason to hope that one brought up in this way would be anything other than a successful pir in the family tradition. It was obvious, he ironically put it, what influence on the mind an upbringing of 'such breadth' would have.[14]

Azad, however, fails to reckon with the education that he did receive. It was precisely that training which helped his father's plans for him to become a pir. Azad later realized the limitations of this education, but it gave him a thorough knowledge of the classical bases of Islam, which, aided by Azad's own intelligence, inevitably made the young boy suspect that there was something strange about the Islam he saw around him. His father's overwrought insistence on his ways could only have further provoked questions in the boy's mind. The elder man was excessive in his acceptance of the adulation of his disciples and equally excessive in his bitter condemnation of 'Wahhabis'. Azad reacted first emotionally, then intellectually:

"Suddenly, when I was at most thirteen years old, my heart became disgusted with my present circumstances and what I saw around me...The unrest increased until I was ashamed by, and despised the things that in other peoples' eyes were so honourabie and estimable. Now, when people kissed my hands and feet, I felt as if some great evil were taking place. A few days before, the very same spectacle had been for me the source of the greatest pride and self-satisfaction!"[15]

Then, Azad describes the next stage, his decision that the beliefs he had been brought up with were 'nothing but taqlid of ancestors, devotion to ancient customs, and inherited dogma'. When he asked why he should believe all this, the only answer he received was, 'Because that is what I was told', or 'Because that was the faith of my fore fathers.'[16] This only raised his doubts further.

Another factor bore upon this situation: the boy's sense of fairness and refusal to accept unearned honour. Azad recalls an incident that helped him to date the revolution in his beliefs, but did not help him to explain it. In fact it explains more than he knew. The incident was a visit to Calcutta by his cousin from Mecca. All the adulation of Khairuddin's disciples was a new experience for this cousin. He revelled in it and actually encouraged it. This was too much for Azad, who felt this was not good. From that time, he began to try and restrain people when they wanted to kiss his feet, and he would go off and reflect for hours on how wrong all this was. He said he did not question the near-worship people gave his father, as he thought that was his right as their pir. What worried him was that they honoured him too, when he was only an ordinary person like the disciples, themselves, and had done nothing to deserve it. After reflection, he was able to support his new conviction . He recalled that the Prophet himself never permitted this kind of thing. He felt that this behaviour was the result of ignorance and that the root of it all was *piri* (the system of honouring and being submissive to pirs). He had come to hate the whole system, in spite of his training and background. Neither his brother nor anyone else understood his thoughts, except for his youngest sister, whose sympathy drew them closer still. He mentioned his thoughts to several others outside the family and found one person who agreed.

Thus in the period of his first exposure to a world wider than his father's house, and while he was still a young boy, Azad experienced a revulsion against the practice of *piri* which was to influence him all his life. It reinforced his growing sympathy for the Wallullahis' teachings, in reaction to his father's narrow and prejudiced views.

Realisation of Inadequacy of Traditional View

Aversion to traditional practices brought him closer to Sir Sayyid, who was a leading Muslim on the path of modernisation. He surpassed the non-conformism of Sir Sayyid and became an atheist so that he gave up the daily prayer also. He is quoted as saying: "After mental struggle of a few days, I resolved once to abjure *namaz* (prayer). O God! I still remember that night, and will never forget, which, because of the mental turmoil that it involved, was equal to a year, an epoch, indeed a lifetime.[17] That gave him mental peace, as if his problem had been solved, without asserting the denial of the religion itself. It soon, however, turned out to be an illusory perception because the turmoil had really gone into the subconscious and returned with an acute sense of void and vacuum and he felt the need to go and kneel before somebody and cry. The Maulana has left behind no account of his struggle with its doubts but has recorded that faith returned with greater intensity, of course, without any conflict with reason. By 1912 he had recovered his faith with realisation of the limitations of the materialist scientific thinking.

Clarion Call to Muslims

With that started a new phase in his life when he launched a pictorial weekly *Al-Hilal* which, on the one hand, created among the religious-minded Muslims a sensitivity about the political problems of the day, goading them to political activism in cooperation with Hindu compatriots and respect for the religion of Islam among the sceptical West-oriented educated class of the community, on the other. The evidence to this is provided by Maulana Mahmood Hasan of Deoband and Maulana Shaukat Ali. The former testified, "All of us were oblivious of our real duty which *Al-Hilal* brought back to us." The latter, an Aligarh graduate, said: "Abul Kalam brought us back to the path of faith."[18]

The objective of the journal was to acquaint the Muslims with what he considered the true spirit of Islam and, on that basis, exhorting them to play an active, indeed leading, role in the national struggle against alien rule. His preference was for cooperation with the countrymen, followers of other religions, rather than co-religionists of other countries. He also opposed the Muslim League policy of separatist Muslim politics and by 1913 was able to bring it closer to the broad nationalist platform of Congress. Of course, he favoured world-wide unity of the followers of Islam in defence of the Turkish Khilafat.

The writings in *Al-Hilal* invited the wrath of the imperialist British bureaucracy. The pro-British daily *Pioneer* of Allahabad accused it of pro-German sympathies and dangerous for the pursuit of war effort. The Bengal government, therefore, invoked the Press Act and forced its closure by forfeiting its security deposit and demanding fresh security, which was beyond its means. In 1916 Abul Kalam started his campaign once again with a similar journal under a new name *Al-Balagh.* In that he announced that he was engaged in translation and exegesis of the Qur'an that they would shortly be published. The readers were asked to send advance subscriptions for it. The entire work was however disrupted by the government ordering his banishment from Bengal and confiscating the manuscripts and some printed forms of both the books. He moved from Calcutta to Ranchi, where he spent three and half years.

Interpreter of Qur'an

During that period he resumed his work on *Qur'an* so that his mission of explaining its meaning in the context of new developments in the world could be brought home to the Muslims. By the time he was released he had completed translation of all the 30 parts and, after return to Calcutta, started preparation for its publication.

Meanwhile he had joined the non-cooperation movement, as an alternative mode of anti-imperialist struggle. This led to his arrest and confiscation of all his papers, including the manuscript ready for press and once again the story of disruption was repeated. The confiscated manuscript was returned on his release but it was so badly mutilated that it could not be printed. It speaks volumes for the perseverance of Maulana as also his sense of the importance of the work for his aims in life that he once again started the translation for the third time. But this time he was so engrossed in political activity that he could publish only the first eight and half parts in 1930; it contains, besides translation of the text, an introduction to the *Qur'an* in the form of exegesis of *Sura Fatiha.* Translation of further nine and half parts was published in 1936. The translation of the remaining parts also had been completed but he could not get it published. Unfortunately, the manuscript could not be traced, after his death, though one of his followers, Ghulam Rasool Mehr, has somehow collected portions of the manuscript and published them. Maulana's work *Tarjman-ul-Qur'an* is considered to be the most important in the literature of Islam and contains essence of his approach to religion, especially Islam and its message for humanity.

While he was detained in Ranchi, Indian politics underwent a radical change. There was widespread disillusionment about the sense of justice and fairplay of the British because of which the Indian political elite had, till then, confined their activity to making demands for associating them with the administration of the country and, extended support to the British in the World War I. The response of the British to these gestures was far from satisfactory. During the war the government used force for recruitment and after the war it was found that all the promises, made to secure Indian support for the war effort, had been flouted. Instead of giving more freedom, even the basic human rights were sought to be abridged with a draconian law, the Rowlatt Act. Even more annoying, especially to the Muslim community was the treatment of Turkey, whose empire was dismembered and it was subjected to severe humiliation. The anger of Muslims was shared by the Hindus also under the leadership of Mahatma Gandhi. The simmering fire was ignited by the brutal massacre at Jalianwalla Bagh and the entire country was up in arms against the British rule. With his call for non-violent non-cooperation, Gandhi showed a new path of struggle which appealed even to those who had earlier been unsuccessfully attempting to build up some kind of insurrectionary movement.

Maulana Azad was among the first to agree with Gandhi and threw himself whole hog into it. He not only joined the Khilafat movement but also Jamiat-ulama-Hind and Indian National Congress. Never a votary of separate political organisation of Muslims, he directed his efforts at bringing the Muslim League closer to Congress. He had succeeded in securing the support of Congress for the Khilafat movement. At Nagpur session of Congress in 1920, a resolution was passed endorsing Gandhi's programme of Civil Disobedience. M.A. Jinnah who till then was among the front line of the Congress leadership dissociated himself from it because he was not in favour of bringing the populace into politics and considered demands, regarding Khilafat, as communal. The movement that was launched created bonds of unity between Hindus and Muslims which was the main theme of the writings and speeches of Azad during the journalistic phase. According to Abid Husain, "The glorious scenes of nationalist fervour and communal unity seen in those days was the fruit of Maulana's written and spoken words."[19]

By the end of that year the Maulana was once again arrested for some of the speeches he had made. He was put to trial before the Presidency Magistrate of Calcutta. The written statement he submitted to the court was eulogised by Mahatma Gandhi, as a fit instrument for political education. It has been published in book form as *Qaul-e-Faisal.*

While he was in jail, the national movement suffered a setback. The non-cooperation movement was withdrawn on account of violence at a place called Chauri Chaura, as Gandhi thought people were not yet morally ready for non-violent struggle. In the midst of demoralisation, consequent upon that the government had succeeded in fanning communal discord which resulted in communal riots in many parts of the country. Besides, the Congress was risen by fierce differences on the question of council-entry. Maulana Azad, after release from prison, devoted himself to the solution of these problems. He was called upon by the Congress to preside over its special session held at Delhi as he had succeeded in bridging the differences between the contending parties. It was a tribute to his sagacity and political skill. He was at that time only thirty-five years of age, the youngest person to occupy that position of honour; not only till then, but till today.

Thereafter the Congress started work on two fronts: to serve common people by securing for them the social equality and improving their economic lot; it adopted a 14-point constructive programme proposed by Mahatma Gandhi in his presidential address at the 1924 session of Congress. It is a significant coincidence that the Mahatma succeeded Maulana in that chair at a time when the national movement was entering a crucial phase to become a mass movement.

After the abolition of Khilafat by Mustafa Kamal Pasha, the Khilafat Conference had lost its *raison d'etre* and was dying. Jamiat Ulama was extending three-way support: for independence to Congress, for Khilafat to Khilafat Conference, and for specific Muslim interests to Muslim League. Azad kept contact with all three, although devoting main attention to the Congress, all the time trying to bring them closer in the interest of broad national consensus and strengthening of the struggle for freedom. Presiding over the 1925 session of Jamiat, he advised it to forget about the revival of Khilafat and directed its efforts to educational, social and economic development of the Muslim community. The Jamiat was convinced by the Maulana, which not only abandoned the idea but complimented Kamal Pasha for the religio-political reforms he had introduced in Turkey. However, Khilafat Committee did not abandon its aim of reviving Khilafat, though paid some limited attention to the constructive activity.

The two organisations, Khilafat Conference and the Muslim League, came close to Congress during the agitation against Simon Commission but drifted away on account of serious differences on the question of Nehru Report which limited its demand to Dominion status, instead of insisting upon complete independence. Maulana Azad, in that situation, severed his relations with both, as in his view there could be no progress of national struggle without the Congress, which was the only organisation based on comprehensive national agenda and not any sectarian issue. However, there was a keen desire in a large section of Muslims to have their own political party. In response to that, Azad launched Nationalist Muslim Conference with the cooperation of nationalist Muslim leaders. It had no separate organisation but provided a common platform for various pro-Congress organisations as Jamiat Ulama, Shia Political Conference, Majlis-e-Ahrar and Khudai Khidmatgar. All of them cooperated with Congress when, in 1930, the party under the presidentship of Jawaharlal Nehru adopted complete independence as its goal, and Gandhiji launched another phase of anti-British confrontation in the form of Salt Satyagraha. Maulana Azad was sentenced to one and a half years of imprisonment. After travelling in the Muslim countries of West Asia and North Africa he had come to the conclusion that the universal core of Islam did provide basis for a world-wide community of Muslims to mould their conduct in accordance with its message but it was no bond for the nationhood. Nations all over the world were based on territory. His contact with leaders of Young Turk movement and the ideas of Kamal Pasha also tampered his thoughts about the system of Khilafat, which could not be treated as a political institution of the world Muslim community. This perspective is quite clearly reflected in all his writings from Al-Hilal to *Tarjaman.* It is necessary to keep in mind this socio-spiritual and intellectual backdrop of Maulana's thinking to correctly understand the course on which his life moved after his release from prison in 1932.

Then onwards till the end of his life, he devoted himself entirely to maintaining the unity in the Indian National Congress, the mainstream of national freedom movement at the time, while trying to bridge the gulf between Hindus and Muslims. In this task he found in Gandhi a kindred spirit. As in the specific conditions in India, Hindus were to play the leading role both in the anti-imperialist struggle as well as in developing relations of mutual confidence with Muslims, the other major community. Maulana Azad always yielded to his judgement even when he held sharply different views, for example the issue of Partition.

His books and writings are fairly large in number. These include: *(1)Elam-e-Haq, (2)Musalman Aurat, (3)Taza Mazamine-Maulana Abul Kalam Azad, (4) Masala-1-Khilafat aur Jaziratur Arab, (5) Qaul-e-Faisal, (6)Khutbat-e-Azad,* (7)*Taqarur*, (8) *Navadir-e-Abul Kalam, (9) Tarjuman-ul-Quran, (10) Tazkira, (11) Azad ki Kahani, (12) India Wins Freedom, (13) Ghubar-e-Khatir, (14) Karawane Khayal, (15) Naqshe*

Azad, (16) Makatib-e-Abul Kalam, (17) Faisla-e-Muqaddama-e-Jama Masjid, Calcutta, (18) *MalirKotla Ka Niza, (19) Sarmad Shahid, (20) National Tahrik (MS), (21) Alberuni aur Gughrafiae Aalam (22) Mutafarriq Khutut.*

Mulana Azad was a patriot, a leader, a philosopher-statesman and a great scholar. By his profound learning and 'luminous intelligence', he did a real good job for Islam, by clearing it of the dust of prejudice and bigotry which had gathered upon it during the eleven hundred years of its history in India. He was a rightful inheritor of all the thought movements of the past. In the unfolding of his intellectual life and in the evolution of his thought, we find staged the whole history of Islamic thought. He was one of the very few acquainted with the philosophies of India and had deep insight into the various religions of the world and could isolate the real and essential from the spurious.

REFERENCES

1. Malihabadi, Abdur Razzaq, *Azad Ki Kahani Khud Azad Ki Zubani* (Calcutta: Daftar Azad Hind), 1960, p. 95.
2. Malik, Ram (ed.), *Ghubar-e-Khatir* (New Delhi: Sahitya Academi), 1967, p. 97.
3. *Ibid.*, p. 98.
4. Malihabadi, Abdur Razzaq, *Zikar-e-Azad* (Calcutta: Daftar Azad Hind), 1960, pp. 116-18.
5. Malihabadi, Abdur Razzaq, *Azad Ki Kahani Khud Azad Ki Zubani, op. cit.*, pp. 187-88.
6. Douglas, Ian Henderson, *Abul Kalam Azad: An Intellectual and Religious Biography* (Delhi: Oxford University Press), 1988, p. 42.
7. Malihabadi, Abdur Razzaq, *Azad Ki Kahani Khud Azad Ki Zubani, op. cit.*, p. 329.
8. *Ibid.*, p. 197.
9. Douglas, Ian Henderson, *Abul Kalam Azad: An Intellectual and Religious Biography, op. cit.*, p. 45.
10. *Ibid.*
11. Malihabadi, Abdur Razzaq, *Azad Ki Kahani Khud Azad Ki Zubani, op. cit.*, p. 235.
12. Malik, Ram (ed.), *Ghubar-e-Khatir, op. cit.*, pp. 252-58.
13. Malihabadi, Abdur Razzaq, *Zikar-e-Azad*, p. 253.
14. *Ibid.*, pp. 243-5.

15. *Ibid.*, pp. 256-57.
16. *Ibid.*
17. Malihabadi, Abdur Razzaq, *Azad Ki Kahani Khud Azad Ki Zubani, op. cit.*, p. 423.
18. Bhutani, Surender, *Maulana Azad and Indian Polity* (New Delhi: Shipra Publications), 2006, p. 18.
19. *Ibid.*, p. 22.

2

IDEOLOGY AND PERCEPTION

Although the overlapping strata of experience in Azad's formative years are not in consecutive periods of time, it is possible to date the quickening of revolutionary political thought in the precocious young journalist, who was secretly harbouring religious unbelief. In his statement before the presidency magistrate in Calcutta in January 1922, he asserted that he was only eighteen years old when he first started speaking and writing on the theme of political freedom. This refers to the year 1906-70 when he had two periods of editing *Wakil*, with a period in between in Calcutta editing *Dar al-Saltanat*. When he first went to *Wakil*, he had the idea that such a paper was the best means to publicize his thoughts so that, when he eventually brought out his own paper, it would immediately have wide influence. He says that *Wakil* had the greatest influence and circulation of any Urdu newspaper, dealt freely with Aligarh matters and Turkish-Egyptian relations, and raised money for the Hejaz railway. Thus, when the first number of *al-Hilal* came out in 1912, he was able to write in the editorial that it represented the coming into reality of a dream that he first had in Amritsar. At the end of 1906, disturbed by news of his brother's death, and pressed by his father, he returned to Calcutta.[1]

In Calcutta, then in the throes of the *swadeshi* agitation against the 1905 partition of Bengal, Azad got a glimpse of the effectiveness of political activism. At the end of his life, he discussed his involvement with Hindu revolutionaries at that time. He was impressed by the revolutionaries' activities, and claimed to have joined one of their groups through the mediation of Shyam Sunder

Chakravarty, an associate of Aurobindo Ghose. In general, Muslims were pleased with the partition, as the government intended them to be, and thus the Hindu activists mistrusted them. Azad, therefore, had a hard time gaining the confidence of his revolutionary associates. Eventually, however, he was able to convince them that it was a mistake to exclude Muslims from their activities, using the examples of Muslim revolutionary struggles in Egypt, Iran and Turkey. He also claimed to have been instrumental in spreading their organization beyond the province of Bengal, so that secret societies were established in Bombay and several towns in north India...just how successful Azad was in convincing his revolutionary friends of Muslim *bona fides* is seriously open to question, however, for one of the major revolutionary groups, the Anushilan Samiti, specifically barred Muslims, while the other, Jugantar, had few, if any, Muslim members. Nevertheless, Azad seems to have had some peripheral association with the political underworld of Calcutta at this time, and later, during the *al-Hilal* period, formed his own religio-political association, the Hizbullah.[2]

It is ironic that, just as Azad was becoming interested in involvement with revolutionary anti-British politics, he was present in Dacca for the inauguration of the Muslim League, with its emphasis on loyalty to the British. The meeting took place on 31 December 1906, and on 25 December Azad wrote to the owner of the weekly *Dar al-Saltanat,* which he was to start editing from mid-January 1907, that he was leaving for Dacca that evening and asking for a month's salary in advance. The presence of the young newspaperman at this historic meeting would explain the later erroneous story that he had joined the League at its first meeting.

The chronology of the next two years is unclear, due to Azad's conflicting accounts. In *Azad ki Kahani,* he says that he worked at *Dar al-Saltanat* for eight or nine months, then rejoined *Wakil.* He had promised to return to Amritsar when he left the first time, and in addition he complained that the owner of *Dar al-Saltanat* did not fake a personal interest in the publication, but allowed the policy of the paper to be influenced by the opinions, of his friends. When Azad returned to *Wakil,* however, he found that because of changes in his own political views, Shaikh Ghularn Muhammad and he could no longer agree. Previously, they had been drawn to each other because of their common devotion to Sir Sayyid. Now, Azad says that 'there had been so many changes in his thinking that recounting them would sound like a whole life history. At any rate, he could no longer stay at *Wakil* but left 'after nine or ten months'.

In *India Wins Freedom,* however, Azad states that in 1908 he made an extended trip to West Asia, including Iraq, Egypt, Syria and Turkey, and was recalled from this trip by the news of his father's illness.[3] Bedar's careful reconstruction of the chronology of Azad's journalistic career states that he spent only a couple of months with *Dar al-Saltanat,* then returned to *Vakil* after eight or nine months in Calcutta, but did not stay with *Vakil* for long.

Azad's connection with the Islamic world of West Asia, of course, was deep-seated. Even though he wrote more about his Indian ancestry, he was proud of his Arab heritage, and regarded Arabic as his mother tongue. He was brought up on stories of his father's exploits in the Hejaz and Constantinople and spent the first ten years of his life in Mecca. He read all the Arabic journals hold all the Arabic books on modern knowledge that he could get hold of. Persian also was part of his literary heritage. Some of his early writings had been about Persian poetry, and this was a special part of his fellowship with Shibli in Lucknow. From Shibli, he would have also heard about the Litter's visits to Turkey, Egypt, and Syria, and contacts with literary figures in those places, including Abduh. He recounts an early introduction to Turkish views from a Turk he chanced to meet in a mosque in Calcutta. He brought him home, where he lived for seven or eight months. This was during the time of Sir Sayyid's influence on Azad, and he says he was impressed to find that this Turk had the same philosophical approach to religion as did reformed Indian Muslims.[4]

Azad had also visited West Asia on more than one occasion following his migration to India from Mecca. He went to Iraq with his brother in 1904, but returned early because of illness. His brother stayed on and visited Syria, Turkey, and the Hejaz, returned to India in ill health, and died young in 1906. In Addition, Azad mentions a visit to Mecca in 1905.[5] Thus, if Azad travelled to West Asia in 1908, it was by no means his first introduction to that part of the world, although it would have been his first visit there as an adult. This time, furthermore, corresponded to his period of rapidly evolving political views. What events, individuals, and ideas did he there encounter which he did not already know from his reading?

He says that he met Iranian revolutionaries in Iraq, and Arab nationalists and Turkish revolutionaries in Cairo, and these strengthened his resolve to arouse Indian Muslims to resist their foreign rulers. He particularly mentions spending a long time in Egypt. It could not have been more than a few months, but one biographer magnified this into a statement that Azad had studied at al-Azhar, a statement repeated by several others. Azad denied this, explaining that he had simply reflected on the education at al-Azhar, noting that it was so hopelessly out of date that Abduh had, in despair, founded another institution, the Dar ul-Ulum, to replace it. The biographer, Mahadev Desai, had misunderstood his point and had assumed that he had studied at al-Azhar.[6] But if Desai was misled, he was not the only one.

Other writers, in commenting on the Egyptian influence on Azad, make such statements as:

At Cairo, where he stayed for some time, he imbibed the spirit of the reformatory movement which had been launched by Syed Jamaluddin Afghani and Shayk Muhammad Abduh...It was the influence of these two great scholars which stimulated the mind of the young Abul Kalam to inaugurate a like movement in his own country.[7]

This statement is apt enough, if the emphasis is on the spirit of the movement, rather than the direct influence of Afghani and Abduh. Ideas such as theirs were 'in the air' at the time, and Azad was doubtless influenced by that atmosphere and the attitudes expressed by Muslims in Cairo, whether his contact was direct or through publications. But there is no basis for the statement that Afghani's 'influence on Abul Kalam Azad was profound'.

To evaluate more carefully the nature of the inspiration that Azad received in, or from, Cairo, one must note his specific reference to the followers of Mustafa Kamil Pasha. They were not the *al-Manar* group, who were mainly Syrian writers, nor were they Abduh's party, but rather rivals to it. Abduh's followers and those of Kamil Pasha 'divided between them the minds and allegiance of educated Egyptians'. Mustafa Kamil's circle held views that contrasted with those of Abduh in their more intense Egyptian nationalism and uncompromising opposition to the British. In a sense, they were all partly indebted to Jamaluddin al-Afghani. He had sought to arouse the Muslim world against the European threat by a revival of Islam as a civilization. Unity was the fundamental theme in all his work. Though he did not deny the importance of national ties and advocated that Muslims co-operate with non-Muslims in the national movements of countries like Egypt and India, Afghani nevertheless emphasized Islamic bonds over and above national patriotism.[8]

Muhammad Abduh, on the other hand, was an Egyptian nationalist, though not a doctrinaire one. He was aware that common history and interests created bonds among people of different faiths who lived in the same country. He emphasized the need for national education; even foreign rule, if it helped in that process, could be tolerated. On this issue, he parted company with Afghani. In keeping with his concern about the tension between Islam and modern civilization, both of which had to be taken into account, Abduh advocated trying to profit from the British presence in Egypt after 1882. The occupation, however, gave nationalist consciousness a new force and produced a new and uncompromising expression of it led by Mustafa Kamil (1847-1908). Abduh and Kamil were politically and temperamentally incompatible. Abduh regarded the younger man as an empty demagogue whose 'Illegitimate' methods were bound to fall. Kamil regarded Britain as the unquestioned enemy. He established his Nationalist Party (Hizb ul-Watan) in 1907, the very year that Abduh's followers founded the People's Party (Hizb ul-Umma). 'Kamil, already master of the students and the street, seemed capable of becoming that of the government, but he died the next year.' Qasirn Amin, one of Abduh's disciples, wrote that he had felt the heart of Egypt beating the day that Mustafa Kamil was buried.[9]

In the year of Kamil's funeral, 'the first great popular manifestation of the new national spirit', the twenty-year-old Azad came into contact with some of his followers. The ideas current among them were not Abduh's ideas in favour of educating Egyptian society in political virtue (which bear some resemblance to Sir Syed's ideas), but rather emphasized the need to generate energy for the struggle against the British. Immediate evacuation without conditions was their motto. Egypt's revival would occur only through her own efforts, especially towards unity, and this could only be based on a patriotic spirit *(wataniya),* as in Europe. Such patriotism could have no limitations of language, religion, or status; it should include all who lived in Egypt, Christian Copts and Muslims alike. There should be no conflict between the spheres of religion and national life; true religion teaches true patriotism. Whether or not Azad heard all these ideas specifically enunciated, they were the kinds of things that Egyptian nationalists were saying and writing at that time. The conservative ulama in Egypt continued to inveigh against nationalism as a concept unknown prior to the western occupation and as a rival to traditional Islamic unity. But nationalism, though European in origin, had become an accepted part of the defense against European domination.[10]

The form of nationalism to which Azad was drawn, therefore, was not the thoughtful, guarded aspirations of Abduh's followers, but rather the vigorous, uncompromising demands of the Kamil enthusiasts. Like all Egyptian nationalists, they envisaged co-operation of Muslims and non-Muslims, but for them the consuming passion was the eviction of the British enemy. Here were Muslims of the same order as the revolutionary Hindus of Bengal. Azad's politics during the *al-Hilal* period, and during his co-operation with non-Muslims in the Congress party, was thus the expression, in the Indian context and at the appropriate time, of the kind of nationalism emanating from Egypt which had impressed him beginning in 1908.

Azad also says that he met in Cairo a group of 'Young Turks', who published a weekly from their centre there, and later mentions the 'Sarruf brothers'. His reference is to the Lebanese writers who produced the newspaper *al-Muqattam* and the monthly *al-Muqtataf,* which he read at the newspaper office in Calcutta. Such Lebanese and Syrian liberals, established in Cairo before the 1908 Turkish revolution that restored the Ottoman constitution, were beyond the reach of the sultan's police and thus able to attack his policies with impunity. From trading the Arab press opposed to the sultan, Azad presumably avoided the kind of unsophisticated equation of 'Ottoman' with 'Islamic' which, characterized the thinking of some other Indian Muslims later during the Khilafat movement. From Cairo, Azad says he then went to Turkey and became friends with some of the leaders of the Young Turk movement, keeping up his correspondence with them for years after his return to India. These Arab and Turkish contacts expressed surprise that Muslims in India were subservient to the British and isolated from the Hindus who were leading the nationalist movement. They felt that Muslims should be in the forefront of the struggle for freedom. These sentiments reinforced Azad's similar feelings and fired his determination to take up this political cause upon his return to India.[11]

In the struggle for national independence, which was the main goal and central concern of his intellectual, journalistic, political and, to a large measure, even of his religious exertions. Azad's life can be perceived in three phases, which retrospectively appear as three stages of his political evolution into an integral personality.[12]

In Phase One: 1906-15 (when his age was 18-27 years) Azad emerges on the Urdu literary and journalist scene as a 'Muslim patriot', imbued with the romantic passion for promoting Pan-Islamic solidarity against the worldwide tentacle of Western colonialism, and for a liberal and rationalist regeneration of global islamic community. In this early phase he drew inspiration from the teachings of three pace-setters of reform in the Muslim world—the islamic revolutionary drive and stirring call renaissance of Asia and the Arab world and its modernization given by Jamaluddin Afghani (1839-97); the intellectual zeal for religious reformation initiated by the Egyptian Mufti, well-known for his liberal and rationalist interpretation of the Quran and the *Shariah,* Muhammad Abduh (1849-1905); and the powerful plea for the urgent reconstruction of Arab polity based on political democracy and creative response to the challenges of the new world made by the fiery Lebanese intellectual, Muhammad Shashid Rida (1865-1935), whose popular journal *Al-Manar,* provided the relevant format for Azad's *Al-Hilal.* This was also the phase when Azad sought inspiration from two of his own Muslim compatriots—Sir Syed Ahmad Khan (1817-98) and Maulana Shibli Naumani (1857-1914). Sir Syed's efforts towards rationalism and modernisation as exemplified in his writings addresses in *Tahzib-ul-Akhlaq. Iafsir-ul-Quran, Maqalat and Khuthet-i-Ahmadiyq,* became a pace-setter for Azad's writings on Muslim social reform, even as Shibli's erudition on a wide range of Islamic studies from the biographies of the Prophet and eminent Muslims to Persian poetry and literary criticism, and above all his humanism, wit and romantic inclinations to life and letters, provided him a breath of new vision and broadmindedness.

However, soon he got disenchanted by Sir Syed's political conservatism and pro-British inclinations. During this phase his, main contribution is as a journalist and an editor, culminating ilk the publication of *Al-Hilal* and *Al-Balagk* which moulded Mus thought and opinion in India. In *Discovery of India,* Jawaharlal Nehru wrote:

> '...Because of his writings he was known in the Islamic countries probably more than any other Indian Muslim...Abul Kalam Azad spoke in a new language to them (Muslims) in his weekly *Al-Hilal.* It was not only a new language in thought and approach, even its texture was different, for Azad's style was terse and virile though sometimes a little difficult because of its Persian background. The older conservative leaders among Muslims did not react favourably to all this and criticised Azad's opinions and approach. Yet not even the most learned of them could easily meet Azad in debate and argument. He was a strange mixture of medieval scholasticism, eighteenth century nationalism and the modern outlook. Abul Kalam Azad attacked this stronghold of conservatism and anti-nationalism not directly but by spreading ideas which undermined the Aligarh tradition...'[13]

In between Phase One and Two, Azad was interned in Ranchi (1916-19). These four years gave him an opportunity for contemplation and reflection and provided the necessary solitude for critical evaluation of his ideas, approaches and assumptions. It was indeed a creative interlude for him. Much of his profound writings like *Tarjuman-ul-Quran* begin in this period, and one finds a great transformation in his outlook on religion and politics, often he comes out of Ranchi.

In Phase Two: 1920-23 (when his age was 32-35 years) Azad appears on the national scene as the leader and ideologue of the Khilafat movement, and with Gandhiji as a pioneer mass mobiliser for civil disobedience and *satyagraha*. It is not adequately recognised that Azad's meeting with Gandhiji for the first time on 18 January, 1920 in Delhi (barely few weeks after his release from Ranchi) was a turning point in Azad's political life. After many hours of personal conversation, partly in the company and in the house of Hakim Ajmal Khan, Azad was probably the first—the very first—person, who fully backed Gandhiji on his newly formulated programme of non-cooperation. He was followed by Hakim Ajmal Khan: Other top national leaders of the time Lala Lajpat Rai, C.R. Das and Motilal Nehru were converted to Gandhiji's way of thinking and strategy of struggle, many months later. At that time Jawaharlal Nehru was still not recognized as the leader of the first rank, nor Vallabhbhai Patel, C. Rajagopalachari or Rajendra Prasad had emerged on the national scene. Of course, Mohammed Ali Jinnah was there, prominent and respected as a top leader, hailed by many, in the words of Sarojini Naidu, as the best ambassador of Hindu-Muslim unity. But it was precisely on this issue of *satyagraha* and mass civil disobedience in 1920, that not only Jinnah violently disagreed, but also left the Congress, never to rejoin it again but to fight against it till the bitter end, in a long drawn battle, in which he castigated the Congress as an Hindu organisation and denigrated Azad as its Muslim 'show-boy'.

It is interesting to recapitulate that Gandhiji's programme of non-cooperation was first presented and endorsed in a predominantly Muslim congregation, presided over by Maulana Azad. This was the Meerut meeting of the Khilafat Committee held in May 1920.

Gandhiji and Azad remained together during 1920 and 1921, while touring the country for popularising the civil disobedience programme. In December 1920, Azad did something reminiscent of mediaeval Indian history, when the Sikh Guru Arjun Dev (1581-1606) had invited the great sufi-saint Mian Meer of Lahore

(1550-1635), to lay the foundation stone of Harminder temple in Amritsar, Azad invited Gandhiji 'as an embodiment of sincerity and sacrifice', to open the Madrasa-i-Islamia in Calcutta, in the Jama Masjid complex on 12 December, 1920. And Gandhiji in his inaugural speech said 'let this Madrasa produce true Muslim and true Indian, ...who would avoid slavery and die for independence'.[14]

In the Third Phase: 1923-58 (i.e., from the age of 35 till his death at the age of 69), covering almost half of his life-time, Azad remained a stalwart of the National Movement and a most eloquent articulator and defender of the values of composite culture and secular nationalism.

In his life Azad travelled on three paths at different times the path of exclusive Muslim patriotism and Pan-Islamism (1906-20); the path of reconciling Muslim patriotism with larger Indian nationalism (1920-23), and the path of thorough going secular, democratic nationalism (1923-58). He traversed all the three paths, as if they were inevitable stages in his evolution has towards the final goal of national independence; as if these phases were unavoidable, obvious and logical for anyone born in a highly traditional and orthodox Muslim family. Maulana Azad symbolized dramatically the entire spectrum of the socialization process in Indian politics that appeared inevitable for a typical Indian Muslim, brought-up in a conventional Muslim environment subscribing to traditional values and norms, heir to inbuilt prejudices and given premises of social life, beginning education in a maktab or a Madrasa circumscribed in his home and family environment by customs, conventions, social attitudes, civic manners, restrictions and taboos. That is, an atmosphere in which every progressive change and attempts at modernisation were decided as slavish imitation of western, rather British and Christian forms and patterns of life, hence repugnant to the dignity of Islam and pride of India. Exposure to Western education was considered a stratagem of enslaving the mind and consciousness of the colonized people thereby vitiating the impulse to revolt against Western-Christian domination. Azad's journey towards secular enlightenment began from such an ascriptive and hide-bound environment. But it is instructive to observe the paradox that exists between Azad born in a traditional household and Jinnah born in a cosmopolitan household, in their trends of political development. While Azad moved from the particular to the general, from the limited to the universal, from sect and community to nation and humanism, from religion-dominated political consciousness to secular, liberal democratic consciousness, Jinnah on the contrary moved just in the opposite direction.

There were four basic assumptions of Maulana Azad's political credo[15]:

(i) that Hindu-Muslim unity is a decisive element not only for national independence but also for building a democratic national identity in India;

(ii) that the Khilafat movement is in essence the struggle for Indian independence and therefore, it was necessary to promote joint Hindu-Muslim via action;

(iii) that non-cooperation and boycott of British goods for the Muslim is not only a political necessity but also a religious obligation, based on appropriate puranic injunctions, whose validity is apparant in the circumstances in which the British government become a belligerent opponent;

(iv) that the building of composite nationalism and stabilising its foundations is not only politically desirable but also a duty of the Muslims, in tune with the injunctions of the *Shariah* and in pursuance of the example set by the Prophet Muhammad himself.

Like Gandhiji, Azad considered Hindu-Muslim unity as an axial principle of national liberation and national reconstruction. For both of them it was an article of faith, a moral imperative. On 25 August, 1921 in his famous address to the Agra session of the Khilafat Conference, referring to Hindu-Muslim Unity, with dramatic emphasis and sincerity he said: 'Friends! if I recognize any work as my life-work, it is this'. And it was in this address probably one of his greatest oration, so compact with new ideas and radical propositions—that he expatiated on the religious dimension of Hindu-Muslim unity. He said: 'If the Muslims of India would like to perform their best religious and Islamic duties...then they must recoganize that it is obligatory for the Muslims to be together with their Hindu brethren...and it is my belief that the Muslims in India cannot perform their best duties, until in conformity with the injunctions of Islam, in all honesty, they do not establish unity and, cooperation with the Hindus. This belief is based on the imperative spirit of Islam'.[16]

As a conclusive religious argument in defence of composite nationalism, he cited the example of Prophet Muhammad himself. In the very first year of Hijra (623 A.D.) the Prophet himself formulated the now famous Covenant of Medina, which was adopted in a general meeting of the people—both Muslims and non-Muslims, as a document declaring that the Muslims ('the Muhajeereen'—the Meccan emigrees and 'the ansaar'—the Medinian helpers) enter into a political compact with the Jewish tribes, the Christians and Sebaens and Pagans, living in and around Medina, for mutual security, aid and support against the belligerent invading tribes from Mecca.

The document enumerated certain items of common concern and common action, and declared that in religious matters, everyone will have his own religion, 'for Jews their religion and for Muslims their religion'. But it categorically stated that all the parties to the Covenant have become *ummat-ul-Wahida.* Maulana Azad explicitly translated *ummat-ul-Wahida* as One Nation: *Umma*—Nation; *Wahida*—One. Other commentators translate it variously as One People, One Community, One Congregation etc. Maulana argued from this innovative, though subsequently unsuccessful experiment of the Prophet in building a multi-religious political community even in his own time, that there is greater and more pressing need for creating a unified nation in India, by strengthening Hindu-Muslim unity and solidarity, and indeed bringing about multi-religious harmony for political unification and nation-building. No one before Azad, nor since, has argued so vigorously from religious angle, about the validity of constructing composite nationalism in India.

Maulana Azad integrated in his personality, deep reflective scholarship of the classical Islamic mould with capacity for rational and pragmatic thinking, attuned to the abiding concerns of social transformation and political emancipation of his motherland.

Maulana Azad remains a shining example of the fusion of the rationalist heritage of Islam and the compassionate heritage of India.

He coalesced with endogenous, creativity the Vedantic vision of many paths to truth with the Islamic doctrines of *Wahdit-e-Din* (Unity of faith) and *Sulhe-kul* (Universal peace).

He could find the echoes of *Vasudhaiva Kutumbakun* in the repeated Quranic message 'the entire Humanity is one community nation'. Indeed in continuation with the intellectual exertions of early pioneers like Al-Beruni, Amir Khusro and Emperor Akbar's great grandson, the heir-apparent of Shahjehan, the Mughal Prince Dara Shikuh. Maulana Azad sought to examine the formulations of Upanishadic speculative thought with the quintessence of Islam, in order to build bridges of understanding between two great systems of social ethics, namely Hinduism and Islam, that dominated the multi-religious scenario of the subcontinent of India.[17]

Maulana Azad's world view is reflected in his monumental work *the Tarjuman-ul-Quran,* Azad argues powerfully about the 'oneness of religious faiths' *(Wahdat-i-Din)* that has been vitiated by the inevitable divergence of *shariah* (laws) necessitated by different socio-cultural environments, and by formalistic and institutionalised schism, promoted by the followers of the diverse faiths. In his monumental commentary on the brief seven verse opening chapter of the *Quran Surat-ul-fatiha,* (which he calls the natural introduction to the study of Quran), Azad emphasises the doctrine of *rububiyat* as the quintessence of Islam in its universal appeal and validity. *Rububiyat* as a doctrine entails the recognition of God as *Rabb-ul-Alameen* (Lord of all Being; author of all Existence, circumscribing all Creation). The word *Rabb*—in Arabic implies 'the Cherisher', 'the Nourisher', 'the Sustainer', 'the Provider' for all His creation. It encompasses the attributes of Brahma, Vishnu and Shiva, in the henotheistic Hindu pantheon.

The system of Divine Nurture *(Nizam-e-Rububiyat)* transcends all divisions and fragmentation of mankind based on any consideration like creed, colour, region, nation, etc. Hence *Rabb* is not the God only of one people, but of all the people. Then Azad emphasises that three attributes of God are reiterated continuously in the Quran, and hence should be recognised as fundamental—namely *al-Rahman* ('the benevolent', *i.e.* one who gives even without seeking) and *al-Rahim* ('the merciful', i.e. one who responds when asked, and is forgiving), and *Malik Yaum-ul-Din* (Master of the day of Judgement, *i.e.* who shall dispense justice). *Providence, Benevolence, Mercy and Justice,* then are the four cardinal *values* inherent in a universal, omnipotent, omnipresent God. Azad lays stress on reason *(aql)* as the instrument of comprehension and explanation of all matters, divine and secular. He concludes his commentary of *Surat-ul-Fatiha* by saying that when such a universal God, *Rabb ul Alameen guides* on the *right path-(ihdenas-Sirat-al-Mustaqeem)* it is not the particular path of any race of nation, but the path on which their is universal consensus of the leaders of all the religions and of all right-minded human-beings, may they belong to any race and any age. Commitment to universal humanism, he says is indeed the essence of the Quranic message.

Maulana Azad is revered without being understood. He remains only partially understood and a much misunderstood personality among the stalwarts of the Indian national movement. Because to a large bulk of our people he has been reduced to a noble 'totem! of the political tribe' called the 'nationalist Muslims'—a tribes whose political legitimacy acquired credence in the pre-partition milieu only as a contra-reference-point to what was then known in the vernacular as the 'League-e Muslims'. Today for most of his compatriots Azad is part of the sentimental heritage of the national movement, a relic, a bygone phenomenon, whose name and memory evokes appropriate sentiments of admiration, veneration, felicitation, adoration, etc, but never of clear and critical understanding, never of rational intellectual comprehension of, his life, his role, his struggles, the lesson of his tragedy, and the abiding message and relevance of his dreams.

One reason for considerable ignorance about Maulana Azad, stems from the fact that in our own time and age, there are not many who can read, much less understand and appreciate the Urdu language in all its powerful thrust, allegorical beauty and sophisticated diction. It is not often realised that the alienation the Urdu language in India, is one of the cruelest cultural tragedies of our times. It has robbed us of a significant part of our heritage, also of the national movement. Most of Maulana's creative works, ideological speeches and journalistic writings, memoirs and account, are almost all in

Urdu. There is not much of consequence, either written or spoken by Maulana, which is available in the English language. Humayun Kabir's English version of Maulana's Urdu narrative—called *India Wins Freedom* is the only readily available book that is read by a large number of people. The book is a reconstruction of Maulana's successive conversations on certain aspects of the last phase of freedom struggle, that is from the formation of Congress ministries in the Provinces in 1937 to Gandhiji's murder in 1948. Stylistically and in emphasis, the book appears more in harmony with Humayun Kabir's Anglo-Bengali assertiveness and occasional blatancy, which makes it a rather sad caricature of Maulana's own Urdu style imbued with subtlety, wit and nuances, and the inevitable grace and generocity, which was integral to his style in life. In other Indian languages what is available is still meagre. Lack of communication is obviously a serious impediment in comprehending a personality. The telling words of a contemporary Urdu poet, Majrooh comes to mind:

> *Zabaan hamari na samjah yahaan* koi *Majrooh,*
> *Hum ajnabi ki tarha apney he watan mein rahey*
>
> (No one here understands my language, O Majrooh,
> Like a stranger, I lived in my own country)[18]

The Maulana was much misunderstood, rather deliberately, by his contemporaries, for variety of reasons—political sectarian, factional and personal. His intellectual brilliance matched with majestic personality, provoked powerful jealously. Admiration slipping into envy, and envy degenerating into hate is not an uncommon psychological passage. In a beautiful fine Ghalib says: 'I have envied beyond limit, that one might suspect it to be hatred'.

The Muslim communalist could not tolerate a man so profound in Islamic theology and ontology, and who was capable of quoting the Quran and the Sunnah in defence of his basic credo of composite Indian nationalism. The orthodox and tradition-bound Ulema were disturbed by his endogeneous, creativity—and rationalist exertion in the interpretation of the faith *(ijtihad-fid-din)* in harmony with the great Hanbali reformer Ibn Taimiyah (1268-1328), who had emphasized God's transcedence to underline oneness of faith

(Wahdat-i-Din) and fraternity of humankind involving reciprocal obligations. Sectarian opposition to Maulana became fierce with his continued affirmation of composite nationalism, not only as a desirable political objective but also as one dictated by rational understanding of the *Shariah* and the Covenant of Medina prepared by the Prophet. His detractors derided *Tarjuman-ul-Quran as 'Congress tafsir'*, and as a *tafsir-bil-ray* (interpretation by personal opinion), in order to prejudice the ignorant Muslim masses from assimilating its great message of reason, humanism and compassion. The Muslim League had wipped-up a campaign of hate against him. In the measure in which Maulana lost his Muslim political constituency, some of the Congress factional groups, tried to weaken his legitimacy and hold.

Azad's fascinating personality had its own points of contradiction as well. There was always an inner tension in his conduct and style and public posture due to dichotomies that his personality had to reconcile. There was the dichotomy between a life of profound scholarship pursuing simultaneously a life of active politics; between involvement in Islamic religious reformation and commitment to secular democratic nationalism; between promoting Muslim mass consciousness on religious symbols and idiom, and yet promoting composite nationalism, involving in its wake struggle against Muslim communalism, sectarianism and separatist politics.

Maulana Azad was one of the greatest intellectuals that the National Movement had produced. His intellectualism was of the classical mould and learning, a real Alim, spanning wide branches of knowledge from Islamic theology to Arabic and Persian literature, *al-kalam,* traditional philosophy and metaphysics, and later his interests stretched to European literature and selective philosophical and scientific studies. Allegorically speaking, one might say that he was a born patrician in an age of plebeian-upsurge, and despite his endeavour to identify himself with the interests and concerns of the plebeians, his in born aristocracy the mind and learning; so evident in his scholarly speeches, profound writings, his style, his manners, his values, that never really get firmly rooted in mass-culture and mass-politics. He was with them, but not of them. He knew it, and never pretended otherwise. There was always a wide chasm between him and his audience. He over-awed them by his oratorical skills, his influency, the flight of his poetic imagination, the flourish of his pen, his learned references and appropriate political fines. Most of his persuasive and erudite Urdu diction, most of the time went over the heads of common mortals, whose elemental response was applause and adoration, without clear understanding.

In the life of nations and civilisation, sometime personalities are also great tragedies. When 'time' and 'circumstance' do not harmonize with the main exertion personality, discordance occurs, which casts a gloom on an otherwise brilliant career. Only those personalities betray the tragic touch, whose previous accomplishments prompt expectations beyond that which can be fulfilled. The element endemic in Maulana Azad's career was due to the fact that he was Muslim in a predominantly Hindu environment, yet bold enough to recommend and propagate composite nationalism to Muslims in variance with the prevalent political consciousness based on communalised politics. But precisely because of this Maulana Azad remains an undaunted symbol of defiance against unreason, sectarianism and parochialism. Whose brilliant exposition remains the heritage of generation which still has to fight the battles he fought battles against communalism hate and violence, for building an enlightened India of his dreams.

REFERENCES

1. Malihabadi, Abdur Razzaq, *Azad Ki Kahani Khud Azad Ki Zubani, op. cit.*, pp. 293-95.
2. Douglas, Ian Henderson, *Abul Kalam Azad: An Intellectual and Religious Biography, op. cit.*, p. 78.
3. Azad, Maulana Abul Kalam, *India Wins Freedom* (New Delhi: Orient Longman), 1989, pp. 5-6.
4. Malihabadi, Abdur Razzaq, *Azad Ki Kahani Khud Azad Ki Zubani, op. cit.*, pp. 212-14.
5. *Ibid.*, pp. 126-28.
6. Desai, Mahadev, *Maulana Abul Kalam Azad: A Biographical Memoir* (Agra: Shiva Lal Agarwal), 1946.
7. Kabir, Humayun, *Mulana Abul Kalam Azad: A Memorial Volume* (Bombay: Asia), 1959, p. 39.

8. Azad, Maulana Abul Kalam, *India Wins Freedom, op. cit.*, p. 6.
9. Douglas, Ian, Henderson, *Abul Kalam Azad: An Intellectual and Religious Biography, op. cit.*, p. 84.
10. *Ibid.*, p. 85.
11. Azad, Maulana Abul Kalam, *India Wins Freedom, op. cit.*, p. 6.
12. Khan, Rasheedudin, "Portrait of a Great Patriot" in Kashysp, Subhash C. (ed.), *Maulana Abul Kalam Azad: A Centaenary Volume* (New Delhi: National), 1989, p. 101.
13. Nehru, Jawahar Lal, *Discovery of India* (Delhi: Oxford University Press), 1982, pp. 346-47.
14. *The Collected Works of Mahatma Gandhi*, Vol. XIX (New Delhi: Publications Division, Ministry of Information and Broadcasting, Government of India), 1966, p. 101.
15. Khan, Rasheedudin, "Portrait of a Great Patriot" in Kashysp, Subhash C. (ed.), *Maulana Abul Kalam Azad: A Centenary Volume, op. cit.*, p. 105.
16. *Ibid.*, p. 106.
17. *Ibid.*, p. 107.
18. *Ibid.*, p. 110.

3

RELIGION AND POLITICS

Maulana's life and thought was all anchored in Islam. When he was publishing the weekly *Al-Hilal,* a reader had written a letter objecting to the mix of religion and politics in its contents. In reply Maulana wrote: "You have, sir, raised an issue that is the foundation of the structure that we seek to build. If you suggest that the arch is not beautiful we might change it, but if you want that the foundation stone itself be changed, we would like to be excused. In our view every branch of human activity has to be seen in the light of religion. Our only asset is Qur'an and we know nothing beyond it. Our eyes and ears are closed to everything else in the world; we have only one beacon light, gifted by Qur'an, and if that is removed we shall be sand blind."

He had claimed: "I have learnt my political ideas from religion. My ideas do not have merely a colouring of religion but are borne of it. Islam brought with it a complete and comprehensive system of rules and there is no human contention for which it does not have a mandate. It is proud of its monotheism and does not like those owing allegiance to it should turn to any other direction. It carries within it a comprehensive system for all aspects of the life of Muslims whether moral or intellectual, political or social, religious or worldly, as rulers or subjects."[1]

From 1910 until his imprisonment in 1921, Azad felt that God had called him to arouse the Muslims of India and persuade them to join the movement for political liberation. On his release in 1923 his political activity continued, but with a significant shift in his conception of his own role. During the period 1910-22, his vision of himself as some kind of a mujaddid or imam, whom God would vindicate in the way. He vindicated the prophets, steadily enlarged. He envisaged leading the Muslims at the head of a 'Party of God' (Wizbullah), which would unite all Indians in ousting the British and enable Muslims to exercise their divinely ordained right to govern. A more sober politician emerged from the Calcutta jail in 1923, ready to work within the normal party structures he had formerly regarded as beneath the dignity of one chosen to be a spiritual successor to the prophets.

Azad considered that his public role had begun in 1910-11, following the restoration of his faith at the end of 1909. During his trial in January 1922, he told the magistrate that "in the last twelve years I have been training my community and my country to demand their rights and their liberty."[2] His political impact on the Muslims of India, however, really began in July 1912, with the first issue of *al-Hilal*. The paper ran for two and a half year, and within that time the shift in Muslim political attitudes was amazing. Azad and his admirers sometimes make it sound as if he were solely responsible. While this is not so, he was nevertheless an outstanding character in the drama. After an interval of a year, he recommenced publication under the title *al-Balagh*, but this only ran- for four months. Years later, a new series of *al-Hilal* ran for six months in 1927. In this latter effort, Azad's name appeared as editor, but the articles were usually unsigned and the main work was done by his associate, Abdur Razzaq Malihabadi. Azad's personal activity by that time was of a different order. The real period of the journal *al-Hilal*, therefore, is 1912-16. Within this short period Azad's achievement was remarkable.

Azad, furthermore, made his technical preparations well. With financial help from his father's disciples, he was able to set up a high-quality press capable of very clear printing in Urdu type and excellent half-tone pictures. He also used the best quality paper. In its attractive appearance, *al-Hilal* excelled Comrade-as Azad no doubt fully intended it should. In addition, with his literary style, Azad clearly mastered the field. Later generations have criticized him for verbosity, occasional obscurity, and his appeal to the emotions rather than to the intellect. After the pedestrian style of ordinary

Urdu papers, however, *al-Hilal* completely swept its readers off their feet. Humayun Kabir has characterized Azad's style as unique in the history of Urdu language and literature, capturing the imagination of the youth of the community with its poetic grace and its formulation of a new faith. This was the greatest appeal of *al-Hilal.* Azad handled current political issues skilfully, sometimes to the discomfiture of his political rivals, but his Journalistic supremacy was based on his powerful style and his religious appeal. *Al-Hilal* spoke in the language of a 'high-souled prophet'; throughout, 'he had the stamp of the mujtahid'. One who later became an admirer, and close associate of Azad admitted that this characteristic at first irritated him. 'This man seems to be making himself out to be a prophet or the *mahdi.*' In any case, the technique worked.[3]

Within the first three months, all the old issues had to be reprinted to meet demands from new subscribers for complete sets. Ultimately the circulation exceeded 25,000. As a religious journal, *al-Hilal* challenged traditional taqlid and offered Azad's fresh interpretation of Islam related to contemporary life. Politically, it challenged the position of loyalty to the British represented by Aligarh. If the intelligentsia were captivated by *al-Hilal's* Urdu style, and Muslim youth were fired by its activist faith, the Deoband ulama recognized the logic of its call to opposition. Azad was disappointed at the slowness of response from the ulama, but no less a personage than the Shaikh ul-Hind, Maulana Mahmudul Hasan, the Principal of Deoband, complimented Azad by noting that: .'We had forgotten the lesson of jihad and Abul Kalam reminded us again.' This was high praise for the twenty-one-year-old editor from a leading alim of India. Even the poet Hall, loyal supporter of Aligarh to the end, wrote Azad a generous letter approving the publication of *al-Hilal.*[4]

Perhaps the testimony of Sayyid Sulaiman Nadwi is most significant of all, because of the surprising bitterness he showed towards Azad for many years. In spite of this, he felt bound to pay tribute to the influence of *al-Hilal.* Recalling the period from *1912* to *1920,* when Muslim politics took a new turn and Hindu-Muslim unity developed, he noted:

"I must in all fairness say one thing. This was the time when Maulana Abul Kalam Azad was bringing out *al-Hilal,* and Muslims were *set* on fire by his passionate words. He sounded loudly and fiercely the trumpet of Jihad, whose name people were afraid to mention, so that the forgotten lesson was on the tongues of people again."[5]

Summarizing Azad's contribution to the new political consciousness among Indian Muslims, one may say that while the annulment of the partition of Bengal and events in Europe showed educated Muslims that old political attitudes needed changing, and the poems and essays of Shibli and others accentuated their disillusionment with the British, those urging that something be done about the situation, pointing the Muslims in the direction of political action, were the editors of *Zamindar, Comrade* and *Hamdard,* and *al-Hilal.* After the outbreak of World War I, all three editors were interned by the British and their papers closed.

Granting the part played by the timing of the appearance of *al-Hilal,* its attractive typeface, Azad's literary style and his skilful handling of political issues, the religious colouring of his political message proved the most effective in generating response. The core of Azad's programme was the inseparability of the religious and political spheres. Commentators credit him with creating, through *al-Hilal,* a consciousness of current political affairs and a desire for freedom in the religious class, and a reverence for religion in the western-educated class. Within the religious sphere, Azad's appeal was remarkably effective. His emphasis on the Quran as a source for guidance in everyday life led his readers to attach renewed significance to the study of the scripture. Azad did not announce specific objectives in the first issue of *al-Hilal* because he wanted readers first to judge for themselves. He said he did not wish to excite the passions of either the westernized leaders or the ulama. But it was soon evident that these two groups were the objects of his special criticism, the one for slavery to the West and the other for obscurantism. He called upon both to bestir themselves to win the freedom represented by Islam and to revive the faith, which was relevant to all aspects of life. His call was also heard by Urdu-reading Muslims outside these two particular groups.

To one who comes to the pages of *al-Hilal* after study of Azad's religious struggles of a few years earlier, the changed style of his writings is very striking. The intensely religious tone of the language in *al-Hilal,* together with the fact that Shibli is on record as having advised Azad to emphasize the picture of himself as a religious man, has led some critics to say that Azad's religion was all a front. Certainly, Shibli knew the value of making religion the basis of political appeal, and he had been a formative influence in Azad's youth. But Azad had left Shibli in 1906 to further his own ambitions and, by 1910, had found his own way back to religious faith. By the time he established *al-Hilal,* Azad had outgrown Shibli, although he still respected him. Letters from Shibli between 1910 and 1913 urge Azad to 'live more and more in the style of religious teachers', and to sound *al-Hilal's* call to total involvement in Islam 'loud and clear'. But the religious nature of *al-Hilal is* not explained by any advice from Shibli; it represented Azad's convictions.[6] Some might still argue, from the fact that Azad ceased to be a fervent Muslim revivalist in the next period of his life, that his stance in *al-Hilal* was not genuine. This raises the question of the development of Azad's religious thought and the meaning of religion in his life. The study of Azad's preparatory years has shown him gripped by a genuine religious experience, and emerging from it with a strong conviction concerning his service, to God and to the Muslims.

The language Azad used in *al-Hilal* was deliberately cultivated, and Azad's style accentuated the religious character of his message. His prose had the cadence of scripture and the emotional content of poetry. His Urdu was replete with Persian and Arabic words, and he frequently repeated the same idea in different ways, emphasizing his thought and showing his linguistic versatility at the same time. He wanted the western-educated to adopt religiously motivated politics like his own. Equally, he wanted to persuade the ulama that he was one of them and to lead them into political involvement. The stylistic affectation of a *fatiha,* or opening editorial written entirely in Arabic, in some volumes of *al-Hilal,* can have no other explanation. The vast majority of his readers might be impressed, but would not understand it. It must have been addressed primarily to the ulama. Later, he used a highly Arabicized Urdu in *Tazkira*, for which, again, the ulama were the audience he had in mind.

In spite of his criticisms of and ambivalent feelings towards the ulama, he still identified with them. His writings make the distinction between the true and the false among them: that if *ulama-e-haqq* and the *ulama-e-waqt,* or the 'devotees of truth' and the 'time-servers'. In arguing with the western-educated, he portrayed the ulama, at least in former times, as profound scholars of philosophy and history. He respected Shibli because he was a well-qualified alim, and he assiduously, though unsuccessfully, sought the co-operation of Sulaiman Nadwi in his various projects, again because he respected his status as an alim. Later during the freedom struggle, he never rebuked his fellow ulama for the way they used religion, with which he could not have agreed. Even though Azad's language was deliberately calculated to impress, we must recognize his stance in *al-Hilal* as genuine.[7]

The Mission of *Al-Hilal*

Azad never conceived of *al-Hilal* as an end in itself, but rather as part of a larger movement. Although he was quite clear about the journalistic goals of *al-Hilal* and was successful in attaining them, he was unclear about the form the larger movement would take. This was primarily because he refused to copy the organizational structures of the modern world and believed that God would 'act in some apocalyptic manner to bring about change. Because of his desire to be involved in some larger work, Azad was anxious, after the journal was established, to hand over the responsibilities of editing to an associate. The man he desperately wanted to take on this responsibility was Sulaiman Nadwi, but he was unable to keep him as a colleague. Azad clearly expected Sulaiman Nadwi to think as highly of his work as he himself did and to be more than ready to edit *al-Halal.* Nadwi declined and left Calcutta. Azad was greatly disturbed and wrote to Sulaiman Nadwi on 9 January 1914:

"*Al-Hilal* was a movement which created a preparedness. But at the same time we must see that this preparedness leads to actual accomplishment. I have definitely decided that, whatever happens to *al-Hilal,* the practical work must be commenced. In fact I have already begun it. In such circumstances it was the end of everything that, in spite of being fully able to, you refused to assist me. Please remember that if, on account of those difficulties and obstacles, I am forcibly restrained and frustrated, then on the day of judgment, it is surely you who will be responsible."[8]

Thereafter Azad repeatedly referred to the possible discontinuation of *al-Hilal.* He professed his desire to continue but confessed that he had become disheartened. His discouragement is further evidenced by the fact that for several weeks no editorials appeared, the number of articles signed by others increased, and double numbers became more frequent. In subsequent issues, however, he acknowledged receipt of letters of appreciation. Then, six months after his chagrin over Sulaiman Nadwi, he announced the decision to publish for eleven months in the year only, adding that he no longer felt obliged to continue making material sacrifices, and increasing the annual subscription rate. Azad saw even routine matters of business, then, in the context of his religious vision. When he felt that God was calling him to some greater work, and the man he considered ideally qualified to take over declined to do so, he seriously believed that man would have to answer at the judgement day for his failure in so great a cause.

The question of *al-Hilal's* continuation was soon answered by government action. Because of its religious nature, *al-Hilal* was allowed to continue publishing with the payment of a security deposit, in spite of its virulent anti-British tone. When Britain went to war in 1914, however, the government took exception to comments concerning allied reverses in Europe. In November 1914, the *Pioneer* of Allahabad published an article against *al-Hilal* entitled 'Pro-Germanism in Calcutta', supposedly at the in stance of the Lieutenant-Governor of the United Provinces. After quoting from *al-Hilal,* the article added that any government that allowed 'unchecked malicious insinuations against British soldiers and sailors', possessed a most 'un-Germanic spirit of toleration'.[9]

The final issue of *al-Hilal* carried a notice giving details of the government action. It announced that on 17 November the Bengal government had forfeited the security deposit of Rs. 2000 and confiscated the double number 16-17 (14-21 October 1914). The government objected to articles entitled 'Military News' and 'The

Fall of Antwerp', as well as a picture of Belgian troops under which appeared the Quranic verse: 'God was not-tyrannical to them, but they were tyrannical to themselves.' Azad was on tour when he heard of the forfeiture and the search of his office and sent a wire ordering the immediate publication of the number being printed. His comment was, 'We shall, with all our might... continue *al-Hilal* and, God willing, shall do so.' In the event, he was not able to do so. The security deposit had been paid, more than a year earlier and, when it was declared forfeit, the government demanded a second deposit of Rs. 10,000. Azad was forced to close the press.

The Hizbullah

Azad's messianic zeal led him to consider his journal and its message as only a part of the larger movement he intended to lead. He knew something of the 'Party of the People' (Hizb ul-Ummah) and the 'Party of the Nation' (Hizb ul-Watan) formed in Egypt in 1907 by the followers of Abduh and of Kamil Pasha, respectively. Now he was going to go one better then either of them. Azad wanted to found the 'party of God' (Hizbullah), with its name taken from the Quran itself. The first hint of this appeared in the issue of al-Hilal for 9-16 April 1913, when Azad commented on a letter he had received from a Lucknow barrister, Mushir Husain Qidwai. Claiming that Turkey was unable to defend Islam and that Mecca and Medina might be attacked by Christians, Qidwai announced plans for an organization to be named the Anjuman-e-Khuddam-e-Ka'aba (Society of Servants of the Ka'aba). It was to be 'strictly religious, having nothing to do with politics', devoted to the service of hajj pilgrims. In the event of a threat to the Ka'aba, however, it would be the basis of a defence organization. Azad noted that he had been aware of these problems, had thought about all aspects of the matter, and had been given a solution by the mercy of God. Details would appear, he promised, in coming issues. In the mean time, Qidwai's letter was published by way of introduction. Later, Azad published further correspondence from Qidwai about the Khuddam-e-Ka'aba, commenting that his own scheme was more comprehensive. In fact, Qidwai launched his organization with the support of

Muhammad Ali and his brother Shaukat, and their spiritual guide, Maulana Abdul Bari of Firangi Mahal, but Azad gave no effective backing to their efforts.

The first actual announcement of Azad's Hizbullah came on 23 April 1913 in an article with the title 'Al-Balagh'(The Trumpet Call), including the Quranic text: 'Answer the call of your Lord before there cometh to you from Allah a Day which there is no averting'. Against the background of Turkey's defeat in the Balkan War, Azad raises the eschatological cry. Alluding to the ascendancy of western military power, he says that the sun has risen in the West, and the door of repentance is being closed. Now is the time for action. He poses a question in bold type: Man Ansari 'Ala Allah (Who are my helpers on the way to God?) and adds in Urdu, Is there anyone therefore ready to go with me? He invites readers to send postcards so that he can prepare a list of mujahidin-e-haqq (warriors for the truth) and jan nisaran-e-millat (those ready to give their lives for the people). The call, he says, is to suffering and not to ease. After a week he announced that 800 names had already been received, that application blanks were being sent with the current issue, and that after another week the 'second stage' would be announced. After two weeks the only further announcement was that some readers had complained about the shortage of application blanks. Others were being printed in books of twenty-five, along with a tract entitled 'The Invitation and the Preaching'. A week later came a notice that the tract and the forms were being printed separately and would be sent upon request.

On 28 May 1913, under the heading 'The Hizbullah and Muslim Women', Azad revealed some of his ideas. A woman correspondent had asked if women were to be included in the Hizbullah. Azad thanked her for her letter and said:

"The call to be helpers of God is nothing other than that Muslims be true Muslims, and a group be created that will be an example in all their actions of the self-sacrificing and soldierly obedience enjoined by Islamic teaching. Resisting distractions from all sides, they will submit their lives to God alone."

In this call, Azad says there is no distinction between men and women:

"In order to bring about changes in us today, an absolutely fundamental principle is that change take place within our homes, and that our women remind us of that voice which we hear outside our homes and, unfortunately, forget. There remains the question of *purdah* (which she had mentioned). It is not related to our point here. Every child of God, remaining in his own place, can meet God. There is no need for him or her to go out."[10]

Early Evidence of National Consciousness

Maulana has also started using his Islamic learning and understanding, both as a matter of faith and as medium for appealing to Indian Muslims, not to hesitate in joining the national struggle against imperialist domination because the struggle was dictated by their faith. He was of opinion that imperialism represented contradiction of Islamic principles of equality and justice. This view had later found expression in his writings but his conviction in united nationalism was evident much earlier. At a time when the British government threw the bait of Bengal partition to drive a wedge in the growing national consciousness, inclusive of all religious communities, the Maulana stood against it and decided to join the anti-British revolutionary movement led by Aurobindo Ghosh and Shyarn Sunder Chakravarty. That movement was suspicious of Muslims and did not admit Muslims into the organisation. Maulana met Aurobindo Ghosh and convinced him to shed the anti-Muslim prejudice because communal unity was essential for the success of freedom struggle. That opened the doors of the organisation for the Muslims.

Another evidence of his commitment to communal unity is provided in his refusal to join the Muslim League when it was founded in 1906. Were he a Muslim nationalist, suspicious of Hindu domination, he would not have opposed formation of a party of Muslims, as he did throughout his life.

His conviction was further strengthened in 1908 when he toured Muslim countries of West Asia and had discussions with the young leaders of those countries. The interaction led to the conclusion that Indian Muslims should be made conscious of their duty as an

Islamic community to join hands with their nationalist compatriots. On return home he began to contemplate on action towards that end. After years of mental cogitation it occurred to him that he should launch a journal to convey the message to the community. He wrote in the opening issue of *Al-Hilal,* "It was the end of the year 1906 when on a wintery night my conscious mind dreamt that as long as the intentions of a person are mere matter of thought and imagination the awakening is no more than a dream. Six long years passed waiting for the realisation of that passionate dream. Throughout that period I remained perturbed by the hopes and aspirations that crowded my mind. Several times it so happened that the mind was overwhelmed by despair and pessimism but by the grace of God determination of mind and blessing of God sustained the hope. And today that dream has found manifestation."[11] Launching the journal was not just an ambitious journalistic endeavour but an advance on the initial expression of nationalistic urge that had driven him to the revolutionary movement.

His close friend and biographer, Abdul Razzaq Malihabadi, reports in *Azad Ki Kahani Azad ki Zabani:* "After return to India I spent some time thinking of the form of action to be adopted and came to the conclusion that a journal is necessary to create public opinion. At that time several Urdu dailies, weeklies and monthlies were published in Punjab and U.P. However, their standard was rather poor; the printing and form were as substandard as the contents. They were printed on Litho and, as such, were unable to print pictures and photographs as was the practice with modern journals. I, therefore, decided that I would bring out a journal that would not only be attractive to look at but also carry high standard impressive articles. In pursuit of the idea I set up the *Al-Hilal* Press and the first issue of the journal appeared in June (July) 1912."[12]

Maulana's sole source of inspiration, we have noted, was Islam as he understood from his personal study. No surprise, therefore, that every issue of *Al-Hilal* was prefaced by a quotation from the Holy Qur'an. This has been used by some students of his life and work to show that, at that stage, he was primarily interested in revival of the religion of Islam rather than promoting the idea of nationalism. Apart from the Islamic flavour of the journal, they adduce his effort to set up an institution to train Muslim scholars to carry to people the message of Qur'an as he understood it.

A more correct interpretation of the ideological framework that Azad was preparing has been given by Rizwan Qaiser in an article *Abul Kalam Azad: Siyasi Zindgi ka Irtiqa* published in a special number of the journal *JAMIA*, where he says that he emerged as thinker who 'prepared for people of India, in particular the Muslims, so that the Muslim community may come into the forefront of the national struggle for independence'.[13] Further on, he points out the difficulties that he might have faced in that endeavour. First, he could not adjust to the contemporary political life because in his family atmosphere there was no scope for politics. Secondly, his experience with the revolutionary movements showed that they were inadequate to satisfy his nationalist political sentiments. At the same time he could not reconcile to either the path of 1857 uprising which lacked a political vision as well as a proper plan of action. Nor could he adopt the advice of Sir Syed who wanted Muslims to keep away from nationalist politics and make friends with the colonial rulers. The politics of Congress, too, was not to his taste because, at that time, it was also a party confined to petitioning the British rather than fighting them.

He had mentally come to believe that overthrow of colonial rule was necessary for which they must join hands with non-Muslim communities. Qaiser, however, falls into an error when he remarks that thereby Azad hoped that the Muslims could regain power and puts him in the category of pan-Islamists. It was not so. The tone of *Al-Hilal* was, of course, such as to push the Muslims into the forefront of national struggle but the tenor of its contents was not to vie with non-Muslims for power but to act as guides to meritorious action as, in his opinion, while Hindus took to national struggle as a patriotic duty for Muslims it was a religious obligation.

Ian Henderson Douglas has summarised the contents of first five editorials of *Al-Hilal* as follows:

1. Complete dependence upon God. It is He who directs the development of the *Al-Hilal* movement and it is His power that will ensure success.

2. The responsibility of 'enjoining the good and forbidding the evil' which is equivalent to '*jihad* in the way of God' in its various forms is incumbent on all Muslims.
3. God in every age chooses and select few of His servants whom He endows with special powers for accomplishing his purposes.
4. The miraculous power, which has already been so amply demonstrated, is no special qualification of the agent (Azad), but lies in the divinely given seed *(Al-Hilal)*.
5. The lines are drawn and the Muslims, as the 'friends of god', must be ready to fight against those who oppose them, 'the friends of Satan'."[14]

Douglas interprets it as the expression of 'growing messianic consciousness of the young Azad of Al-Hilal'. He perhaps does not know that all the leaders of Indian nationalism were using religious symbols to rouse their communities neither to be treated as prophets or messiahs but to join the common struggle to build a united Indian nation and confront the British, who were misleading them into believing that India was not a Nation but conglomeration of religious communities, essentially in conflict with one another. For example, Gandhi, who was nearest to Azad in politics, also not only used religious symbols but also invariably presented his political proposals as divinely inspired.

We have already seen that his understanding of Qur'an and its message was neither sectarian nor blind traditionalism; indeed, he had revolted against this thinking of the guides and mentors of Muslims including his own family and launched upon discovering the soul of religion that could solve the riddle as to why the people of the same faith and different communities created by the same power fought against one another. It is that meaning and understanding which he wanted Indian Muslims to comprehend and reject the enticements of those who either wanted them to shun politics or to form separate political party of Muslims and wholeheartedly plunge into the struggle for national independence. That was his mission which he passionately adhered to throughout his life. People with full and unflinching faith in God are bound to believe that the mission they are pursuing is not their personal discovery but the gift of the Creator. Indian nationalism and its promotion was, as such, an integral part of his faith.

How should he serve the mission? His rejection of the existing political avenues had led him to the journal as medium which, he used with telling effect. The journal could not be all and end all for its message was for action and he had to give lead in that direction and not leave the recipients of the messages to their own fate.

Let us sample some of the passages from the journal. In one of the issues he writes:

> "Where can I find the trumpet whose sound should awaken 40 crore people from deep slumber? How shall I impart that strength to my hands whose beats may rouse the careless ones from dreams of death? ... Robbers are beating at the city doors and the citizens are busy whining and wailing; the robbers have broken the locks and yet the house-owners are sleeping! ... O you who think this weeping is your courage and who deem despair as life, what is this that your house is on fire, the wind is fanning the flames but none among you has water in hand? And, if you were just waiting for this moment, don't you think the time has come? If you were waiting for the boat to sink, don't you see it is on the brink?"

"It is not a simple call, it is a veritable whiplash to force Muslims to rise in revolt against the Government and snap connection with the separatist tendency induced by Aligarh movement. Notice this, for example:

> "No evil influence of a community can avert the inevitable event and the day is bound to arrive when there will be a final revolution in India, the fetters of slavery that it has worn will drop down under the impact of the strong winds of freedom that 20th century has brought with it and the inevitable will be accomplished. Suppose at that time the history of the country's development is written, do you realise what would be written about the role of seven crore human beings? It would be

recorded that there was an unfortunate community that proved a hindrance to country's progress, misfortune for its well-being, a millstone in the way of independence, plaything in the hands of rulers, an instrument of gambling for the strangers, a deep wound on India's forehead and a heavy stone in the hands of Government to crush the aspirations of the country. And, it will be added with deep regret that this happened to be the community of Muslims that had a great history of human dignity and majesty, that had been gifted the legacy and leadership of the world, that was sent down to liberate God's Creation from oppression and exploitation!"[15]

These are prophetic words reflecting the understanding of historical forces. Having administered a strong slap, he conveys the warning:

"If you wish that history of India should mention you as dignified people, let me read the writing to you. There would certainly be a chapter about you but do you know what it would contain? It would record that India progressed on the road to national advance and independence; the Hindus moved ready to sacrifice all but these unfortunate creatures went and hid themselves in caves, the former called them but they sealed their lips!"[16]

And thereafter is administered direct advice:

"Innumerable nights of negligent intoxication have passed and now, for God's sake, raise your heads and see that the sun has risen. See how far your fellow travellers have travelled and where you are stuck. Don't forget that you are Muslims and Islam makes lot of demands on you.... Remember, for Hindus, struggle for freedom is a part of patriotism but for you it is a religious obligation and struggle in the path of God (*jihad*)...."[17]

Never would he miss an opportunity to rouse the sentiments of Muslims against the British rule and, towards that end, shook their conscience as well as reminded them of the sacrifices and great deeds of their forbears.

It is significant that all these moves and various political activities of Azad were initiated before the emergence of Gandhiji on the political horizon. Advent of Gandhiji into the National Movement and Azad's meeting with him had crucial bearing on the future course of the Movement. Azad met Gandhiji on 18 January, 1920 at the residence of Hakim Ajmal Khan in the presence of Lokmanya Tilak and Ali brothers. Personally also, it was a turning point in Azad's life. Azad was meeting someone who could understand his language and perception and with whom he could share his aspirations and agonies.

Before his meeting with Gandhiji, he defined collective identity of the Muslim community in terms of Islam and defined and visualised a safe and legitimate place for the Muslims within the subcontinent. In Gandhiji he found institutional support for his political stand. The Khilafat Movement, and later the Non-cooperation Movement, was to provide a broader platform and offer more serious challenges to Azad's , budding political career.

Azad, with his belief in international Islamic Brotherhood, was concerned with the socio-political problems of the Muslim all over the world. When the British Empire threatened the Turkish Caliphate, which, according to Azad was the symbol of unity of the Muslim world, Azad wanted to mobilize the Indian Muslim opinion in support of the Caliphate. The programme of Hindu-Muslim co-operation visualised by Gandhiji diverted the Khilafat Movement into the channel of the Nationalist Movement. With the involvement of the Congress under Gandhiji and Azad's leadership, the Khilafat Movement reached out to all sections of the Muslim society, and mobilised them as an elemental force which shook the edifice of British rule to its very foundations.

Yet another turning point in Azad's political career was marked by the Non-co-operation Movement launched under the leadership of Gandhiji. It was during the Non-cooperation Movement that he began to think of Hindus and Muslims as forming one nation. Until this time Azad was a member of both Congress and the Muslim League. But after the League at its session of 1921, denounced the

Civil Disobedience Movement, Azad along with several other prominent Muslim leaders, left the League for good.

He exhorted the Muslim masses to join the freedom struggle by giving a religious justification for the Movement: For the Hindus working for independence might be a patriotic gesture, but for the Muslims it is a religious duty.[18] In the 1920s, Azad was, to a Large extent, responsible in sanctifying the Hindu-Muslim partnership and in drawing more and more Muslims to the fold of the Congress, thus enhancing the momentum of the Freedom Movement.

In 1923, at its Delhi Special Session, he was elected President of the Indian National Congress at the age of 35, becoming the youngest Congress President to date. He was an ardent protagonist of Hindu-Muslim unity On his election, he said:

> "If an angel were to descend from the high heavens and proclaim from the heights of the Qutab Minar: 'Discard Hindu-Muslim Unity and within 24 hours Swaraj is yours', I will refuse Swaraj but will not budge an inch from any stand. If Swaraj is delayed it will affect only India, while the end of our unity will be the loss of our entire human world".[19]

During this period he also came into contact with Jawaharlal Nehru and established a personal rapport with the latter which continued for the rest of his life. Azad drew inspiration from his association with Gandhiji and Nehru and inspired them too in turn. He had nothing but ungrudging praise for Nehru and also touched on the points where they agreed to disagree. Both of them didn't hide anything from each other and were equally aware of the evil designs of the British in sowing the seeds of communal discord in India which subsequently led to the trauma of partition.

The National Movement entered a new phase in the 1930s posing a novel challenge to men like Azad who were wedded to the concept of united India. After the heady days of the Khilafat and Non-cooperation Movement, Hindu Muslim unity proved unequal to the challenge of devising a constitution acceptable to all the classes and communities within the country.

Indeed, although the 1930s again witnessed a country-wide agitation against British imperialism, Muslim participation in the agitation was not as conspicuous a feature of resistance as was true a decade earlier. Maulana Azad was the most prominent among the Muslim leaders who remained loyal to the cause of a united Hindu-Muslim struggle against British imperialism at this crucial juncture.

At a time when many Indian Muslims led by the Muslim League were crying for partition, Azad stood up in defence of the unity of the subcontinent. When the Congress launched the *Satyagraha* Movement in 1930, Azad was again arrested. He was a party to every direct action launched by the Congress during the course of the Freedom Struggle and spent 11 years of his life in British jails. He accepted the most challenging assignment of his life when he took over the presidentship of the Indian National Congress at its Ramgarh Session in 1940. Gandhiji whose nominee, Pattabhi Sitaramayya, lost to Subhas Chandra Bose, wanted to have a consensus candidate. The entire left in the Congress with the exception of M.N. Roy supported Azad. Mahatma Gandhi observed thus on Azad's election: '... that he (Azad) is, today, the supreme head of the Indian National Congress, has deep meaning...'[20]

Shortly before Azad presided over the Ramgarh Session of the Congress in 1940, Nehru said of, him: '....be is not the type of man who like's the rough and tumble of politics. He is very sensitive and rather avoids crowds and publicity. He lacks a certain vital energy. In a wider world he is rather out of place as he thinks on political lines and hardly at all on social or economic lines... In the Muslim world of India he is tremendous in advance. Probably he is the ablest among the Muslim divines. Most of them are afraid of him because he can floor them in any argument. His knowledge even of the scriptures and traditions is very great'.[21]

It was this greatness that Maulana carried to the office of the President of the Congress at a crucial juncture. He, said on his election:

"Eleven hundred years of common history (between Hindus and the Muslims) have enriched India with our common achievements. Our languages, our poetry, our literature, our culture, our art, our dress, our manners and customs, the innumerable happenings of our daily life, everything bears the stamp of our joint endeavour. There is indeed no aspect of life which has escaped this stamp. Our languages were different, but we grew to use a common language, our manners and customs were dissimilar, but they acted and reacted on each other and thus produced a new synthesis... This joint wealth is the heritage of our common nationality and we do not want to leave it and go back to the times where this joint life had not begun. If there are any Hindus amongst us who desire to bring back the Hindu life of a thousand years ago and more, they dream, and such dreams are vain fantasies. So also if there are any Muslims who wish to revive their past civilisation and culture which they brought a thousand years ago from Iran and Central Asian they dream also and the sooner they wake up the better. These are unnatural fancies which cannot take root in the soil of reality. I am one of those who believe that revival may be a necessity in a religion but in social matters it is a denial of progress.

"This thousand years of our joint life has moulded us into a common nationality. This cannot be done artificially. Nature does her fashioning through her hidden processes in the course of centuries. The cast has now been moulded and destiny has set her seal upon it. Whether we like it or not we have now become an Indian nation, united and indivisible. No fantasy or artificial scheming to separate and divide can break this unity. We must accept the logic of fact and history and engage ourselves in the fashioning of our future destiny."[22]

It should be noted that these observations were made at a time when fanatic elements had already started weaning the Muslim masses away from the National mainstream. This is an analysis coming out of what Nehru said, 'a mind as keen as razor's edge' and of strong commonsense, with 'a vast fund of knowledge'.

His tenure as Congress President was longest in its pre-independence history. He presided over the Congress during the most crucial phase of the struggle. It was under his presidentship that the All India Congress Committee passed the famous 'Quit

India Resolution' and gave the call of 'Do or Die'. The Movement was ruthlessly suppressed by the British Government and Maulana Azad, along with the rest of the Congress leaders, was arrested and put behind the bars.

On his release in 1945, he was entrusted with the most delicate task of negotiating with the British and the Muslim League for transfer of power to Indians. He negotiated with Lord Wavell, the Viceroy of India. Later, at Shimla, he led the Congress delegation in talks with the Cabinet Mission headed by Sir Pethwick Lawrance, the Secretary of State for India. He wanted to have a dialogue with Mohammed Ali Jinnah who, in his characteristic arrogance, brushed him away and refused to talk to one he considered as the 'Congress Show boy'.

However, he pulled through these turbulent times. He had to face the might of the apologists of the British Raj as well as the proponents of the vivisection of thc subcontinent. He did it with equanimity and stoicism and without losing poise or dignity. Maulana Azad carried the Congress with him through these historic six years with matchless grace and distinction. He also consistently tried to heal the rift between the Congress and the League. If he failed, it was not for want of trying or for lack of political skills. The communal schism baffled even the great Mahatma, who attempted in vain in the 1940s to achieve what he successfully did during the Khilafat and the Non-cooperation Movements.

Maulana was an intellectual 'par excellence' and a political giant. Above all he was an uncompromising patriot. Azad's writings and activities reflect a synthesis of his political/nationalist philosophy and his religious philosophy. Though they are saturated with a religious fervour it is easy to discern the secular message from between the lines. He wanted to act as a scholar disseminating ideas through the instrumentality of his writings, among the Muslim religious teachers whom he regarded as natural leaders. He thought that it was the educated class that ought to be educated first so that they could influence the behaviour of the general public.

REFERENCES

1. Malihabadi, Abdur Razzaq, *Azad Ki Kahani Khud Azad Ki Zubani, op. cit.*, p. 36.
2. Azad, Mualana Abul Kalam, *Qual-e-Faizal* (Calcutta: al-Balagh Press), 1922, p. 67.
3. Kabir, Humayun, *Mulana Abul Kalam Azad: A Memorial Volume, op. cit.*, pp. 69-78.
4. Douglas, Ian Henderson, *Abul Kalam Azad: An Intellectual and Religious Biography, op. cit.*, p. 100.
5. *Ibid.*
6. Ikram, S.M., *Modern Muslim India and the Birth of Pakistan* (Lahore: S.M. Ashraf), 1965, pp. 128-129.
7. Haq, Mushir-ul, *Muslim Politics in Modern India* (Meerut: Meenakshi Prakashan), 1970, pp. 132-33.
8. Douglas, Ian Henderson, *Abul Kalam Azad: An Intellectual and Religious Biography, op. cit.*, p. 104.
9. Desai, Mahadev, *Maulana Abul Kalam Azad: A Biographical Memoir, op. cit.*, p. 38.
10. Douglas, Ian Henderson, *Abul Kalam Azad: An Intellectual and Religious Biography, op. cit.*, pp. 116-17.
11. Bhutani, Surender, *Maulana Azad and Indian Polity* (New Delhi: Shipra Publications), 2006, pp. 88-89.
12. Malihabadi, Abdur Razzaq, *Azad Ki Kahani Khud Azad Ki Zubani, op. cit.*, p. 36.
13. Bhutani, Surender, *Maulana Azad and Indian Polity, op. cit.*, p. 90.
14. Douglas, Ian Henderson, *Abul Kalam Azad: An Intellectual and Religious Biography, op. cit.*, p. 114.
15. Faruqi, Ziya-ul-Hasan, *Mulana Abul Kalam Azad Towards Freedom* (Delhi: B.R. Publishing Company), 1997, pp. 90-100.
16. *Ibid.*
17. *Ibid.*
18. Kashysp, Subhash C. (ed.), *Maulana Abul Kalam Azad: A Centenary Volume, op. cit.*, p. 10.
19. Zaidi, A. M. and Others, *The Encyclopaedia of the Indian National Congress*, Vol. VIII (New Delhi: S. Chand and Company), 1980, p. 612.
20. *Ibid.*, Vol. XII, p. 335.
21. *Ibid.*, p. 225.
22. Presidential Address at the Fifty Third Session of the Indian National Congress, Ramgarh March 1940 in Malsaini Arsh, Abul Kalam Azad (New Delhi: Publications Division, Ministry of Information and Broadcasting, Government of India), 1976, pp. 133-156.

4

CONCEPT OF NATIONALISM

The main features of Maulana Abul Kalam Azad's nationalism were his deep faith in the principles and practices of Islam and equally deep commitment to India, its destiny and integrity. Its quintessence is eloquently expressed in his presidential address at the Ramgarh session of the Congress in March 1940. "I am", he stated, "a Muslim and profoundly conscious of the fact that I have inherited Islam's glorious traditions of the last thirteen hundred years. I am not prepared to lose even a small part of that legacy... As a Muslim, I have a special identity within the field of religion and culture and I cannot tolerate any undue interference with it. But with these feelings, I have another deep realization, born out of my life's experience, which is strengthened, not hindered by the spirit of Islam. I am equally proud of the fact that I am an Indian, an essential part of that indivisible unity of Indian nationhood, a vital factor in its total make up without which this noble edifice will remain incomplete. I can never give up this sincere claim."[1]

Despite its passionate articulation as in Ramgarh, his nationalism was technically not a product of primary attachments which, in the words of Clifford Geertz, "meant one that stems from the ' givens'—or, more precisely, as culture is inevitably involved in such matters, the assumed 'givens'—of social existence: from being born in a particular religious community, speaking a particular language, or even a dialect of a language, and following particular social practices. These congruities of blood, speech, custom, and so on, are seen to have an ineffable, and at times overpowering, coerciveness in and of themselves. One is bound to one's kinsman, to one's neighbour, one's fellow believer, *ipso facto*, as the result not merely of personal affection, practical necessity, common interest or incurred obligation, but at least in great part by virtue of some unaccountable, absolute import attributed to the very try itself."[2]

Azad's nationalism could not have been the result of birth and language. He was born in Mecca; his mother was an Arab. They spoke Arabic at home. Azad learnt Urdu, though very early in his life. This raises the question whether his nationalism was of kind Ernest Gellner had in mind when he wrote, "Men do not in general become nationalists from sentiment or sentimentality, atavistic or not, well-based or myth-founded; they become nationalists through genuine, objective, practical necessity, however obscurely recognized."[3] Azad's nationalism could not have been based on 'practical necessity' felt in terms of personal interest. Rather, one can argue that his personal interests would have been better served had his stand on nationalism been in tune with that of the bulk of Muslims in pre-Partition India who thought that they constituted a distinct nation by virtue of their religion and could not remain a part of a Hindu-majority India. While he was a respected leader in independent India, he might have become the undisputed leader of the subcontinent's Muslims had he supported the separatist line of the Muslim League. For none of the latter's leaders had his stature as an Islamic scholar and his charisma.

If a feeling of necessity led Azad to express his pride in being "an essential part of that indivisible unity of Indian nationhood", it was born of his realization that Partition would adversely affect the interests of Muslims as well as India as a whole. His attitude towards Partition becomes clear from his deposition before the Cabinet Mission in 1946, "I have examined its (Partition's) likely effect upon the fortunes of Muslims in India.... I have come to the conclusion that it is harmful not only for India as a whole but also for Muslims in particular. And in fact it creates more problems than it solves.... Two states confronting one another offer no solution to the problem of one another's minorities but only lead to retribution and reprisals by introducing a system of mutual hostages.[4]

This realization could not have come in a day. It was clearly the result of what he calls his "life's experience". In order to understand the nature and ingredients of the latter, one has to view it in the context of the events of his life (1888-1958) unfolding in a tumultuous period marked by the emergence and growth of two major forces in India-Muslim politics and the national struggle for independence. He was deeply involved in both which were shaped not only by their mutual interface but the forces released by the conflict between nationalism and separatism within Muslim politics, nationalism and colonialism and Islam and colonialism respectively in the matrix of contemporary history.[5]

A major factor in the shaping of his outlook on life was his family background. His father, Maulana Khairuddin, was a scholar in his own right and was perhaps the first Indian to deliver a series of *wa'az* (discourses) inside the holiest precincts of Islam. Both his parents came from families of highly respected Islamic scholars. This as well as the rigorous education he had from his very childhood in all aspects of Islamic thought and practice made sure that his entire *weltanschauung,* covering a wide territory from his ethical, political and social beliefs to the contours of his personal culture, was strongly rooted in his understanding of the teachings of the Quran.

Not surprisingly, Azad's feeling of nationalism and opposition to British rule was deeply rooted in his profound and abiding faith in Islam. This becomes clear if, among other things, one looks at *Qual-e-Faisal* (The Last Word), the written statement he presented on 24 January 1922, before the Chief Presidency Magistrate, Calcutta, in whose court he was being prosecuted for his role in the Khilafat movement. Syeda Saiyidain Hameed, sums up the essence of his position when she writes, "Islam does not sanction any form of Government unless it is based on freedom (*Azadi*) and democracy (*jamhooriyat*). Islam has been revealed to mankind to restore the lost freedom of the human race. It has established the supremacy of *haq* (truth) and denied the right to any except Allah to hold sway over the human race. It has introduced the concept of equality among human beings and forbidden any differentiation on the basis of race, colour or nationality."[6]

Clearly, Azad's understanding of the political implications of Islam in the context of British rule in India was very different from that of, say, Sir Syed Ahmad Khan, the founder of the Aligarh movement and other Muslim leaders who collaborated with the British. This is because his understanding of his religion was deeply influenced by his own personality, which again owed its basic orientation to his being a rebel from a very early age.

His rebelliousness was perhaps a result of the resentment he felt against the rigorous and joyless upbringing that his father had prescribed for him. He chafed at being educated at home, at generally not being allowed to go out of the house except for a short period in the evening, and the stem ways of his father. The result of this as well as his extraordinary intellect, and the profound scholarship he had acquired at an astonishingly early age, was the interest he took in Urdu literature (his poetry was much appreciated when he was very young), his learning of how to play the *sitar,* his learning of English and clandestine subscription to Sir Syed Ahmad Khan's *Tezib-ul Alhlaq*—all of which was severely frowned upon by his father and, finally, by his giving up offering the *Namaz*.[7] His rebelliousness, however, did not take him outside Islam. Rather it prompted him to view the latter in the light of reason. His emphasis on rationality was clearly reflected in his laudatory references to the Mutazila, which lie described as the most successful sect in Islam because of its contribution to the establishment of *Aqliyat* (rationalism) in Islamic literature and the introduction of the study of philosophy and science, in the August-September issue of the *Lisan-us-Sidq* (Voice of Truth) which he had established in November, 1903.

A tendency to rationally interrogate the world around one often leads to reform. Not surprisingly, *Lisan-us-Sidq* was set up to effect, among other things, social reform among the Muslims. For this, Muslims had to understand the real message of the Quran. Not satisfied with the manner in which the latter's message was being conveyed to them in India, he began writing the *Tarjuman-al Quran* (Spokesman of the Quran) an Urdu translation of the Holy Book with "his commentary on the opening *Surah Fatihah* and its themes—Divine Providence, benevolence, justice, unity and guidance, *rabubiyah, rahman, adala, tawhid* and *hidaya*".[8]

Mushirul Hasan gives an excellent idea of Azad's religious profile when he writes that the Maulana "was the product of an intellectual and cultural milieu that was unmistakably Islamic, a curious but fine blending of the Arab, Turkish, and Indo-Muslim traditions. He rejected dogma, rituals and *taqlid* but did not tear himself apart from his socio-cultural moorings which bore an Islamic stamp. The Islamic component—not in a narrow, sectarian sense—was thus an essential feature of is personality, the springboard of his intellectual activities."[9] There was, however, little trace of blind faith or bigotry in his religion. He once wrote in *Al-Hilal,* a political periodical he established in Calcutta in 1912, "The greatest hindrance to human religious progress is unquestioning acceptance of traditional beliefs ... the first thorn of doubt that pricked my heart was against *taqlid* (following authority without question). If the foundation of belief should be knowledge, why on *taqlid* and inheritance.[10]

Azad's interpretation of the Quran led him to a theory of inter-religious amity. His religious conviction centred on a belief in *wahadat-e-deen* or the essential oneness of all religion. Speaking at Santiniketan on the occasion of Visva Bharati's inauguration as a central university, he said in 1951, that Tagore's conception of God rose "above all narrow limitations of race, religion or creed" and added that the term *advaita* (non-dualism) would, translated into Arabic, read *"Wahdahu la Sharik,* the One who has no second, which is the highest affirmation of the monotheistic belief."[11] Once one arrives at such a view of religion, one can hardly argue that people professing different religions belong, to different nationalities. This was the fundamental reason for his differences with Mohammad Ali Jinnah and other Muslim League leaders who demanded Pakistan on the ground that Muslims formed a separate nation by virtue of their religion which determined their nationality. His position on the matter is clear from his observation, "It is one of the greatest frauds on the people to suggest that religious affinity can unite areas which are geographically, economically, linguistically and culturally different. It is true that Islam sought to establish a society which transcends racial, linguistic, economic and political frontiers. History has, however, proved that after the first few decades or at most after the first century, Islam was not able to unite all the Muslim countries on the basis of Islam alone." [12]

If anything, it was that fraud which was the result of necessity felt in a most narrow and selfish way. According to Paul Brass, "Muslim leaders in North India in the late nineteenth century did not recognize a common destiny with the Hindus because they saw themselves as losing their privileges as a dominant community..." Hence they chose to emphasise "a special sense of history incompatible with Hindu aspirations and a myth of Muslim decline into backwardness."[13] Azad's role in national politics was also determined by his fierce hatred of the British which was the result of several factors, including his coming into contact with the followers of Mustapha Kamil in Egypt where he arrived in 1908 in the course of his travels, which also covered Iraq, Iran, Syria and Turkey. Kamil, who died the same year, and who had set up a nationalist party, Hizbul Watan, in 1907, was a staunch opponent of British rule and wanted its immediate and unconditional end. He believed that Egypt's revival had to be based on an upsurge of patriotism that transcended the barriers of language, religion and status, and included all inhabitants of Egypt—whether Muslims or Christian—copts. Azad, who had earlier come into contact with the revolutionaries of the Jugantar and Anushilan groups in Calcutta who came into prominence during the struggle against the Partition of Bengal (1905), was strongly influenced by Hizbul Watan's nationalist creed and deeply stung by the surprise Arab and Turkish nationalists expressed over the Indian Muslim's indifference the nationalist struggle.

Gandhiji's blend of Khilafat and Non-cooperation was the realisation of Maulana's search for a mode of political activity that could promote cooperation among different religious communities of India and bind them together as one nation. It was his conviction that such a unity was essential for the success of struggle for independence. As an Islamic scholar he had found sufficient evidence in the Qur'an and the practice of the Prophet for joining hands with those non-Muslims who caused them no harm and sought their cooperation as was the case with the bulk of Hindu population who had joined Gandhi in the struggle against British imperialism that had betrayed its promises to Turkey and its Khilafat. He was quite conversant with the opposition to Turkish Khilafat among Arab nationalists as well as the attitude towards it of Kamal Ataturk, the father of Turk nationalism. Yet, in the specific circumstances of India, he considered it good enough cause to mobilise Muslims to join hands with non-Muslim compatriots to work for freeing the country from the imperialist yoke, especially when Congress had been persuaded to approve the programme of Gandhiji at the Nagpur Congress.

Those who think that he had changed from a pan-Islamist to a nationalist ignoring everything that Azad had been doing till then. Way back in the first decade of 20th century he had tried to persuade Aurobindo Ghosh to admit Muslims into the *Anushilan Samiti* which till then carried the prejudice that Muslims were loyalists and were averse to any anti-British movement. He had refused to support the Partition of Bengal which was a British device to create a gulf between Hindus and Muslims and his writings in *Al-Hila.* Five, clearly show that he did not want Muslims to keep away from the national struggle; on the other hand he was warning them of being left behind in shame while the caravan of nationalism was destined to go ahead and succeed.

He did use Quranic quotations in support of his argument that Muslims did not have to learn lessons of freedom and equality from non-Muslims as they were the chosen people of the Almighty to make human freedom and equality prevail. Their keeping aloof from national struggle was therefore betrayal of their Faith and the commandments of God. The argument was for Azad, both a matter of Faith and a strategy, to wean the community away from Sir Syed's path of seeking favours from the British by professions of loyalty. He had himself rejected that path though he had admired Sir Syed's departure from tradition to understand Islam in the light of rational and naturist view.

His support to Khilafat was thus no dogma as it was for several other Khilafatists who looked upon it as an exclusively religious movement. He never failed to stress in his speeches upon the essentially political nature of the movement. As Ian Douglas has pointed out "Azad was never as carried away emotionally by the idea of Turkish Khilafat as the Ali Brothers and some other enthusiasts were. He knew the writings of Arab nationalist opponents of the Ottomans too well for that. He was fully prepared to throw his weight behind the Khilafat movement, however, when he saw how it could serve the cause of Indian nationalism, and especially when, after the September 1920 session of congress it had the support of that body as well and: 'Nationalism and Khilafatism were now organically related as the avowed twin objects of the entire country'."[14]

Douglas, however, is not convinced that Azad had succeeded in evolving an ideological framework for nationalism from the Qur'an because, in his later political speeches he referred more to the historical role of Muslims in India rather than Qur'an as he did in his speeches in Khilafat conferences. It is the error of expecting theology in political discourse addressed to common gatherings as distinct from Khilafat conferences where the audiences were almost exclusively Muslim.

Douglas admits that "He was concerned with the great evil of denying human freedom and, there could be no question in his mind that God and his eternal truth were on the side of the oppressed."[15] In July 1920, a Khilafat conference at Karachi had issued an edict for Muslims to boycott services in the British army. Maulana Azad supported that edict in his articles in the *Paigham*, a journal edited by his associate, Abdurrazzaq Malhabadi, in which he exhorted the Muslims to join Gandhi's movement because 'no Muslim can be subject of a rule that has denied its freedom to religion'. Paying fulsome tribute to the leaders of Khilafat movement, Ali Brothers and Husain Ahmad Madni who had pronounced that edict and had been arrested, Azad wrote:

"We have no regret over their arrest. Rather we should be envious of the honour thus conferred upon them and show greater enthusiasm for the cause. Earlier when they had been arrested I had ruefully said that they had beaten me in the race. Today, instead of feeling regretful we shall congratulate them for taking the lead over us."[16]

Azad had never missed an opportunity to rouse the Muslims for rising in revolt against the British rule; it was the theme of all his speeches in the Khilafat conferences. His regret was that he was denied the honour that had been conferred on the participants of the Karachi conference. His desire was fulfilled when the Non-cooperation movement was withdrawn by Gandhiji in the wake of some violent incidents because he wanted the participants in the movement to strictly observe non-violence. Maulana Azad and C.R. Das declared a hartal in Calcutta to protest against the arrival of the Prince of Wales. The government unleashed a reign of terror in Calcutta and Maulana Azad was arrested on charges of sedition. The charges were framed on the basis of a CID. report according to which he had, in a conference, tried to rouse the Muslims telling them that they should not cooperate with those non-Muslims who had targeted their religion and by this he meant the British.[17] He had in fact, in the presence of Gandhiji, tried to convince the Muslims that "they had adopted non-cooperation not because of Gandhiji... and stressed that Khilafat and non-cooperation are truly Islamic issues. It is just a coincident that his principles of non-violent non-cooperation and that Muslims are grateful to their Hindu brethren who had endorsed it."[18]

In a message to the people before arrest he said that his expected arrest was a matter of triumph because what he could not accomplish through his speeches would be accomplished by this action of the government. The affidavit he submitted before the Calcutta Presidency Magistrate is a declaration of defiance, a cogent indictment of the unjust position of the government.

The hearing of the case started on 11 January 1922. Maulana Azad presented his case in Urdu language and desired that he should be allowed to submit the translation, which was conceded. This was a way of expressing lack of confidence in the honesty of official translation. Thus the affidavit in English was filed on 24 January. The last day of the hearing was 9 February 1922. Before that he issued a press statement saying:

1. Nobody should come to see the court proceedings on 9 February. Nor should there be crowd on the roads.
2. It is certain that he would be punished. The public should wait for the verdict patiently and peacefully. There should neither be a hartal nor any demonstration.

3. On 9th people should not gather near the prison, nor try to see me. The normal activity should be continued and intensified."

The magistrate in his verdict, sentenced him to imprisonment for one year. Not unexpected! In his affidavit Azad had declared that he did not expect justice from the official courts in the prevailing circumstances. Indeed, his statement in the court was a severe indictment of the judicial system. He had stated:

"The list of judicial injustices is pretty long. History has not been able to adequately condemn it. We see in it pious ones like Jesus who had been put up in contemporary court along with thieves. We see here the fate of Socrates who was to drink poison just because he was the most truthful person of his age. We, see, too the Florentine devotee of truth Galileo...The good and the evil are put up among the accused...Standing here in the dock as criminal. I feel that I am the envy of the kings."

Azad did not deny, indeed declared that he was fighting against the British government in pursuit of the sacred cause of freedom and national rights and that he was trying to sow this seed in the minds of his compatriots:

"I am the first person among Indian Muslims who, as far back as 1912, called upon the community to commit this crime and within three years changed its slavish mentality which the government had cunningly induced into it. If the government considers me a criminal and wants to punish it is not something unexpected which should be a cause of complaint for me."[19]

Elaborating the background of his arrest he told the court that the government did not like the call for hartal that he had given along with Mr. C.R. Das and in turn had unleashed a reign of terror: "When I saw that the government, unable to thwart the hartal, had become mad with rage like a person in fury who can commit any outrage any time...All the national volunteer organisations have been declared illegal and strict orders are in force against all public gatherings. In this situation my duty was quite clear...Freedom of speech and expression and association are the birthright of every individual. According to the famous philosopher Mill, their violation is nothing short of massacre of humanity and this was being openly violated. I, therefore, cancelled all my outside programmes and decided to stay in Calcutta till the government withdraws its communique and order or arrests me."

Roundly condemning the government, he declared:

"This government is an evil and an evil should either be reformed or destroyed...Why do I and millions of my countrymen believe so? ...I would say that it is my belief because I am an Indian, because I am a Muslim and because I am a human being."

Continuing his statement, he explained the Islamic tenets which called for freedom of which the only alternative is death. He also clarified his difference of opinion with Mahatma Gandhi that, unlike Gandhiji, he did not believe that violence should not be confronted with violence in any situation but I agree with him in the specific case of India and am convinced that India would triumph through non-violent struggle and its victory would be the victory of moral force.

Concluding his statement in the court he addressed the magistrate with these words:

"Mr. Magistrate I will not take more time of the court. It is an interesting but instructive chapter of history which both of us are putting together. In this I am in the dock and you, on the magisterial seat. I agree that for this task that chair is as necessary as this dock. Let us quickly finish this memorable task that is like fiction. The historian is waiting for us and future has been looking to us since long. Let us come here at short intervals and you also write your verdict speedily. This will continue for some time till the doors of another court open, the court of divine dispensation. Time will write the verdict and that will be final."[20]

More than Defiance, a Precious Document

Maulana's statement was a brave act of defiance but more than that it was a valuable contribution to people's political education. Not only did it constitute a more powerful inducement to the Muslim community to enthusiastically participate in the national struggle against colonial tyranny but provided the most cogent and convincing arguments for non-violent non-cooperation movement. The evidence of this is the reaction of Mahatma Gandhi, the moving spirit behind that movement, who wrote:

"I have received a copy of the affidavit that Maulana Azad has submitted in the court. The statement is a great literary piece; besides fluency, it has compelling passion and ardour. It is courageous, unflinching and uncompromising while retaining sobriety and seriousness of tone. The whole statement from beginning to the end produces enthusiastic excitement and it seems Maulana is presenting an address on Khilafat and Nationalism."

After reading the statement as the dawned upon me if clear significance of the boycott of courts. I felt if we had not taken the step wherefrom would we have acquired the strength and fearlessness that is working in us.

The impact of the boycott of courts should not be assessed only in the number of lawyers giving up practice. The real impact is seen in the absence of the crowds inside and outside the courts that was seen two years ago. They are now the resort of money-lenders and gamblers. Neither are they the source of national independence nor assurance of individual freedom. How rapidly the nation is advancing can be gauged by seeing the sentiments of the brave and fearless hearts.

Although his words are directed towards the court but he is in reality addressing the people of the country. His statement indeed gives the impression that he is expecting severest punishment.

What a statement he made after hearing sentence of a year's rigorous imprisonment: 'This is much below my expectation of punishment!"[21]

Gandhi's reaction provides the evidence, if evidence was at all required, to show that he was a nationalist par excellence; and not because of any influence of Gandhiji. In fact, for him India's national struggle was the key to freedom of humanity from imperialist oppression and tyranny which had characterised Indian nationalism as distinct from chauvinist nationalism of imperialists and fascists, the world over. He genuinely believed this nationalism to be the lesson of Islam in contemporary situation.

Beyond Khilafat

The agitation for ending the Khilafat wrongs was not the be all and end all for Maulana Azad. He had plunged into it because he saw in it the potential opening for creating the atmosphere for struggle to build a national force by welding together various religious communities that the British were pitting against one another to thwart the movement for national independence that was taking long strides, especially after World War I. He was also conscious, more than many others, that it might not last long. That is why when Gandhiji proposed withdrawal of the agitation in the wake of some violent incidents, while he and his Bengal colleagues were in Calcutta jail, he was the only one to agree with the proposal.

A short while after the withdrawal of agitation came the news that the Sultan and Caliph Waheeduddin had been deposed by the Turks and Abdul Majid has been named Caliph, but divested of secular powers. There was mixed reaction to this step of Mustafa Kamal who was being supported by the Khilafatists. Jamiat Ulama Hind refused to believe the news and blamed Reuter news agency for misinforming the world. In their opinion separation of religious and secular powers of the Caliph was transgression of Shariat. There were others, Hakim Ajmal Khan and Dr. M.A. Ansari among them, who were happy with the development for, as against hereditary power, election of the Caliph was more in line with the practice followed immediately after the demise of Hazrat Mohammad.

Maulana Azad tried in his own way to make sure that the Muslims of India, as a reaction to Turkish developments might not drift away from the path of nationalism on which the Khilafat movement had brought them. In his presidential address at the Kanpur Conference of All India Khilafat Conference he appealed not to sentimentally react to the events in Turkey and said that the real focus of the Khilafat Committee should be on political mobilisation of the community. He pointed out that the Khilafat Committee members were superior to others because of their conviction that the aims of Indian independence and composite nationalism are interlinked. They should not stray from this belief and refuse to become tools in the hands of the alien rulers like some self-styled leaders of Muslims.

The Maulana perhaps had in mind the background in which the Turks had taken the harsh step against the nominal Caliph. In November 1923 Sir Agha Khan and Syed Amir Ali had sent a joint letter to Esmat Inonu, the Prime Minister of Turkey, posing themselves as friends of Turkey and warning him of the strong adverse reaction to their treatment of Caliph among the Sunni Muslims. In the said letter they had advised him 'the Grand National Assembly should so maintain the Khilafat as to safeguard the confidence and honour of the Muslim nations'. The letter was mischievously released to the press and was seen as the Turkish government as a conspiracy to incite the Muslim world against them in the name of the Caliph. Hence they decided to do away with the institution once for all.

He, therefore, advised the Muslims in his Kanpur address to leave the Turks to their fate; rather than carry with futile struggle in the cause of Muslims in other countries, they should adopt a programme for positive action for the progress of their own country so that their place in the national movement and in the future free India is ensured.

It was a timely advice. Khilafat movement had united the Hindus and Muslims. As the movement petered out, there was revival of the atmosphere of hatred and enmity with the reactivation of *Shuddhi* and *Tabligh* movements with consequent communal violence in different parts of the country. The atmosphere of communal harmony that was seen between 1919 and 1925 began to be overwhelmed by disunity and discord.

The years during which Azad wrote and published the two volumes of his Tarjuman were a period that was politically unrewarding for him. For Indian Muslims generally, the period following the collapse of the Khilafat movement was a time of uncertainty. From 1930 onwards, growing communal disorder jeopardized Hindu-Muslim unity in the eyes of many former nationalist Muslim leaders. Nothing moved Azad from his conviction, however, even if it meant standing alone. After 1937, he became the leading Muslim in the Congress, and in 1939 he was elected its

President, a post he held throughout the war years. By that time, the Muslim League under the leadership of Jinnah was becoming a force in Indian politics, having taken full advantage of Muslim grievances against the Congress provincial governments that came to power following the elections in 1937. After the Muslim League's Lahore Resolution of 1940, which committed the party to the demand for Pakistan, Azad became a target of attack; as a symbol of those Muslims who wanted a united India, he was an obvious irritant to the Muslim League, which claimed to speak for all Muslims in the country. Muslim papers that supported the League wrote inflammatory and threatening articles against him. He was accused of being a 'dishonest traitor to Islam' and a 'mercenary agent of the Hindus'.[22]

This was not a time, Mujeeb comments, 'in which moral values could be asserted in the form of political principles'. Nevertheless, Azad's political activities continued to be inspired by his religious faith, even though he now learned how to 'eliminate irrelevant religious considerations when thinking of or discussing purely political issues'. In other words, Azad had advanced beyond the kind of religious motivation he had advocated in the *al-Hilal* period, when he claimed that the Quran gave specific guidance on all political Issues. In his youth, Azad had been totally inexperienced in politics. Now with a full knowledge of what was involved, he had proved that his religious faith could guide him in the area of general principles, and give him strength for the difficulties he had to face. He earned a reputation for 'absolute impartiality' and 'unimpeachable integrity' which served him well particularly in the years after independence.[23]

As for the policy of Hindu-Muslim unity in a united free India, on which he was at variance with the Muslim League, he no longer argued for it on the basis of the Quran and sunna as in the Khilafat days. He shared with the ulama of Deoband and the Jamiat ul-Ulama-e-Hind three general reasons for opposition to the Muslim League and the Pakistan idea: first, the ulama *felt* that they represented the longest Islamic tradition of opposition to the British in India; second, they distrusted educated League leaders and felt they were not Islamically motivated; finally, they were concerned about the position of, Muslims who would be left in a predominantly Hindu India if a separate Pakistan were formed.[24]

When Azad later stated his reasons for supporting the Congress and rejecting the idea of Pakistan, his primary argument was in terms of the best interests of the Muslims. He wrote of safeguarding their future, and said that the Pakistan solution would not remedy the ills of Muslims. Significantly, he did not repeat his earlier argument that, in Quranic terms, Hindus were not aggressors against Muslims, and so Muslims should follow the example of the Prophet's covenant with the non-Muslims at Medina. Such arguments would not have been convincing in those days of communal antagonism. In a statement on Pakistan issued in 1946 at the time of the Cabinet Mission to India, his main emphasis was on the practical results he foresaw. He comments on the Muslim League scheme:

"I have examined its likely effect upon the fortunes of Muslims in India...I have come to the conclusion that it is harmful not only for India as a whole but for Muslims in particular. And in fact it creates more problems than it solves...Two States confronting one another offer no solution to the problem of one another's minorities, but only lead to retribution and reprisals by introducing a system of mutual hostages.

Elsewhere in this remarkably prescient statement, Azad says that the whole idea of dividing territories into 'pure' *(pak)* and 'impure' goes against his grain, and repudiates the very spirit of, Islam. In support of this, he quotes the hadith: 'God has made the whole world a mosque for me.' He regarded Pakistan as 'a symbol of defeatism...a confession that Indian Muslims cannot hold their own in India as a whole...a sure sign of cowardice.' This is entirely consistent with his position in *al-Hilal* that Muslims should be involved in nationalist politics, not out of cowardice and not because they are aping the Hindus, but because it is correct in Islamic terms.[25]

After the formation of Pakistan, Azad cited the lessons of history which taught that Islam, on its own, could not unite all Muslims into one state:

It is one of the greatest frauds on the people to suggest that religious affinity can unite areas which are geographically, economically, linguistically and culturally different. It is true that

Islam sought to establish a society which transcends racial, linguistic, economic and political frontiers. History has however proved that after the first few decades, or at most after the first century, Islam was not able to unite all Muslim countries into one State on the basis of Islam alone.

He also doubted whether East and West Pakistan could overcome their differences and become one nation, but further said that Pakistan was a fact and that India and Pakistan should develop friendly relations and co-operate with one another.

This statement is highly significant for understanding Azad's religious and political thought. It represents a historical realism which recognizes the need for the co-existence of religions in civil polities. Azad no longer on specific Quranic arguments, but, all the same, he remained faithful to his larger Islamic instincts.

If Azad's nationalism was the product of any feeling of necessity, it was that of liberating India from British rule and maintaining the country's unity which, he felt, was essential for the well-being of both Hindus and Muslims in the subcontinent. He strove until the very last to prevent India's Partition and was a very sad man when his efforts failed. At a time when religious fundamentalism of several types are increasingly active threatening the country's territorial integrity and the secular fabric of its life, Indians, particularly Hindus and Muslims, need to know more about what he stood for and what kind of a country he wanted India to be. They will find in his writings a breadth of vision, an erudition and the stamp of wisdom that will not only be rewarding in itself but will help understand our contemporary history better. As important, they will be better acquainted with a highly sensitive scholar-statesman who was also a great patriot who declared stridently, "Because I am an Indian, I am a Muslim, I am a human being."[26]

REFERENCES

1. Presidential Address at the Fifty Third Session of the Indian National Congress, Ramgarh March 1940 in Malsaini Arsh, *Abul Kalam Azad, op. cit.*, pp. 133-156.

2. Clifford, Geertz (ed.), *Old Societies and New States: The Quest for Modalities in Asia and Africa* (New York: Free Press), 1963, p. 108.
3. Ernest, Gellner, *"Nationalism" in Thought and Change* (Widenfeld and Nichalson), 1964, p. 159.
4. Hasan, Mushir-ul (ed.), *Islam and Indian Nationalism: Reflections on Abul Kalam Azad* (Delhi: Manohar), 1992, p. 25.
5. Karlekar, Hiranmay, "The Nationalism of Mulana Abul Kalam" in Singh, Mahavir (ed.), *Mulana Abul Kalam Azad. Profile of a Nationalist* (New Delhi Anamika), 2003, p. 96.
6. Hameed, Syeda Saiyidain, *Islamic Seal on India: Independence, Abul Kalam Azad – A Fresh Look* (Karachi: Oxford), 1998, p. 120.
7. *Ibid.*, p. xii.
8. *Ibid.*, p. 20.
9. Hasan, Mushir-ul (ed.), *Islam and Indian Nationalism: Reflections on Abul Kalam Azad, op. cit.*, p. 83.
10. Douglas, Ian Henderson, *Abul Kalam Azad: An Intellectual and Religious Biography, op. cit.*, p. 76.
11. *Ibid.*, p. 241.
12. Azad, Maulana Abul Kalam, *India Wins Freedom, op. cit.*, p. 248.
13. Brass, Paul, *Language, Religion and Politics in Northern India* (Cambridge: Cambridge University Press), 1974, p. 124.
14. Douglas, Ian Henderson, *Abul Kalam Azad: An Intellectual and Religious Biography, op. cit.*, p. 177.
15. *Ibid.*
16. Bhutani, Surender, *Maulana Azad and Indian Polity, op. cit.*, p. 103.
17. National Archives of India, Home Pol. D. 29 October 1920.
18. Bhutani, Surender, *Maulana Azad and Indian Polity, op. cit.*, p. 104.
19. *Ibid.*, pp. 107-108.
20. Azad, Mualana, *Abul Kalam, Qual-e-Faizal, op. cit.*, pp. 1, 19-20.
21. Bhutani, Surender, *Maulana Azad and Indian Polity, op. cit.*, pp. 107-08.
22. Mangolori, Tufail, Ahmed, "Musalmanon Ka Raushan Mustaqbil" in Hussain, S. Abid (ed.), *The Destiny of Indian Muslims* (Bombay: Asia), 1965, p. 555.
23. Mujeeb, M., *The Indian Muslims* (London: Allen and Unwin), 1967, pp. 440-42.
24. Faruqi, Z.H., *The Deoband School and the Demand for the Pakistan* (Bombay: Asia), 1963, pp. 110-21.
25. Azad, Maulana Abul Kalam, *India Wins Freedom, op. cit.*, pp. 142-45.
26. *Young India*, February 23, 1922.

5

NATIONAL EDUCATION

Maulana Abul Kalam Azad, the first Education Minister of India, organized his efforts to rebuild India's tradition of cultural appreciation by laying down the basic pattern of education amidst the practical problems arising in the process of achieving independence and to create the basic infrastructure on road to educational development. The coherent and consistent evolution of his ideas regarding education, fusing the Islamic, the Indian and the Western into a single pattern is worthy of investigation and evaluation in depth. His most significant contribution to education is the broad democratic humane, balanced vision, which he brought to bear on the entire edifice of education. That way the basic objective of this chapter is to explore the ways through which Maulana Abul Kalam Azad attempted to legitimize the newly emerging Indian state to the Indian society.

Democratization of Education

One of the classics of the literature on the relation between education and stratification is Max Weber's typology of educational systems, which is based on the idea that the structure of domination defines the ends and therefore, the criteria of selection. Weber viewed that "Historically, the two polar opposites in the field of educational ends are: to awaken charisma, that is, heroic qualities or magical gifts; and, to impart specialized expert training. The first type corresponds to the charismatic structure of domination; the latter type corresponds to the rational and bureaucratic (modern) structure of domination. The two types do not stand opposed, with no connections or transitions between them. The warrior hero or the magician also needs special training, and the expert official is generally not trained exclusively for knowledge. However, they are polar opposites of types of education and they form the most radical contrasts. Between them are found all those types which aim at cultivating the pupil for a conduct of life, whether it is of a mundane or of a religious character. In either case, the life conduct is the conduct of a status group".[1] Weber generalized that modern societies have conflicting definitions of education in terms of "cultivated type of man" and the newer concept of the specialized "expert". However in either type, education serves the purpose of domination.

Alternatively, social selection through education can be related to trend towards increased universalism, which focuses upon the trend from ascription to achievement in socially selective processes. In fact democratization of education starts from this perspective of achievement orientation. The question arises: how does one start this process, or expedite it in regions where it has already been started? The question becomes more important in the context of the leading ideas of the nationalist elite at Independence which can be summarized under these headings: sovereignty, unity, order, a strong state, secularism, democracy and parliamentarianism, economic self-sufficiency, and the need for social and economic reform.[2]

Maulana Azad pin-pointed his efforts for the democratization of education through which he wanted to universalize 'achievement' as the basic criterion in the social selection processes and thereby wanted to break the domination structure of hierarchical Indian society. Maulana Azad put into operation programmes of social action designed to release more fully the democratic ideals that lie at the base of our tradition. One may identify four such programmes, which were put into operation:

(a) Removal of illiteracy through universalization of elementary education up to secondary standard and a drive for adult education including education for women;
(b) Equalizing educational opportunities in Indian society where exploitations on the basis of class and caste divisions were rampant;

(c) Three language formula where the state languages and Hindi would be the medium of instruction but English will remain as an important second language;
(d) Sound primary education throughout the country.[3]

Azad viewed, "Every individual has a right to an education that will enable him to develop his faculties and live a full human life. Such education is the birth right of every citizen. A state cannot claim to have discharged its duty till it has provided for every single individual the means to the acquisition of knowledge and self-betterment." He was convinced that "regardless of the question of employment the state must make available to all citizens the facilities of education up to the secondary stage."[4]

Azad held that in independent India the planning of education on the national level was even more important than economic or industrial planning. If educational training was unable to inculcate the right values and ideals, the security and welfare of the state would be in jeopardy. He laid down a detailed programme of universal education. The centre of activity was to be the village school. In 1948 Maulana Azad put forward the idea of spending on education "at least 10 per cent of the Central revenues"[5] a dream, which is yet to be realized in India. Azad was successful in framing the official policy of instituting special stipends and scholarships for students coming from backward classes. In his survey of Azad's role in 'what he called democratization of educational opportunities' through the installation of scholarships for the students of the backward classes, Professor Saiyidain remarked that the provision on this head went up "about 75 fold, from 3 lakhs in 1944 to 2.25 crores in 1960.[6] While advocating a complete change to Indian languages as the medium of instruction Azad always spoke of the need to maintain English as important second language, since its importance as an accepted international language was undeniable. He viewed, "I am convinced that national interests demand that every pupil in the secondary stage should study three languages compulsorily. He must study first his state language, second Hindi, if it is not the state language and third English. If Hindi is the state language he must study another language."[7]

Azad acknowledged that the ultimate success of any educational programme depended on proper education of women. As he put it if women took to education more than half of the worlds problems would be solved as educated mothers meant literate children.

Last but not the least was his emphasis upon sound primary education and adult education. He viewed that with the extension of democracy the problem of adult education had become even more important than it was in the past. In his view "Adult education has two aspects, viz. (a) arrangements for making the adult literate, and (b) the provision of measures to enlarge their minds and enable them to take an intelligent interest in the affairs of the country."[8] As for the primary education he wanted to make it free, compulsory and universal. Since the villages contain the maximum population of India Azad wanted to make primary education village centric. He also wanted to make primary education audio-visual although it did not tally with the real life situation.

Promotion of the Basic Ideals of Democracy Through Social Eduation

Azad understood that the retention after independence of the British colonial administrative system as well as many of the numerous rules, regulations and acts introduced by the British Raj to govern India, obviously favour the domination, in national politics and national administration, of the elite social groups of diverse castes and creeds brought up and nurtured in the colonial educational traditions. Until and unless this structure of domination is broken, the upliftment of the socially backward classes, their participation in the politico-administrative processes cannot be ensured. Hence Azad was interested to establish the congruence of the formal democracy as a constitution for popular government and real democracy in the sense of actual participation of the people in the government. To that end Azad envisioned a basic pattern of social education for all, which laid the foundation of India's development programmes. He made a distinction between Social Education on the one hand and sociology and social welfare on the other. To him Social Education constituted "a course of study towards the production of a consciousness of citizenship among the people and the promotion of social solidarity among them."[9]

As he viewed there are five basic elements contained in Social Education:

(a) Every citizen must know the meaning of citizenship and the way democracy functions.
(b) There must always be instructions in the laws of personal and public health. True citizenship implies knowledge of and respect for the laws, which govern the health of the community.
(c) Social education must also mean imparting of such information to the people as will enable them to effect some improvement in their economic status.
(d) Social education involving as it does improvement of bodily and mental health cannot ignore the proper training and refinement of emotions. Art and literature are instruments of this training.
(e) Social education should also contain on element of instruction in a universal ethic, with special emphasis upon the necessity of toleration of one another's differences in a democracy."[10]

Thus through this social education policy Azad opened up the horizon of a real participatory society. He understood that society would seem to itself to be much more participant, If the actions actually performed by the officials are seen as having been done at its own instigation and for its sake, and are therefore, accepted by the people as being in some extended sense of their own. It is largely a matter of social psychology but is grounded on the peculiar logic of the concept of action.

Promotion of Mutual Understanding and Harmony

Democratic thinkers have always argued that democracy is a way of life, which goes beyond the structural ensemble of institutions, and upholds a culture of tolerance and accommodations of different views. Rajni Kothari in one of his articles wrote, "The striking thing about India's historical culture is the great variety and heterogeneity that it has encompassed and preserved. This is owing to many reasons the diversity of ethnic and religious groups that have come in succession and settled down, the eclectic rather than proselytizing style of spiritual integration characteristic of Indian tradition, the absence of either a unifying theology or a unifying and continuous secular traditions, and above all, highly differentiated social system that has brought functional hierarchies, spatial distinctions and ritual distances into a manifold frame of identifications and interdependence."[11] The result of all this has been 'a continuous pattern of co-existence between diverse systems and lifestyles.'

Azad understood that in such an essentially plural society an element of mutual understanding and tolerance should always be upheld through institutional education. In his inaugural address at the UNESCO Seminar on 2-11-1949 Azad spoke that "India had been at her best when the doors were wide open to all who came from abroad. She partook of whatever lessons the world had to teach and equally freely gave the world her best." The acceptance of unity in diversity has been her motto throughout the ages. The essence of this principle is a large and wide-hearted toleration in which differences are recognized and given their due. The Indian genius has always recognized that 'truth has many facets and conflict and hatred arise because people claim a monopoly of truth and virtue.'[12]

Azad was always in favour of tethering the State to a secular policy in view of deep religious susceptibilities of the people. At the same time Azad was profoundly clear in upholding that secularism has no apathy to religion. Indian way of life has been moulded for centuries by the traditions of religion. Hence, Azad viewed that it would be impossible to have an intellectual mould without religion. But he held that the State should supervise religious instruction so as to ensure that adherence to religion did not degenerate into intolerance, bigotry and communal violence. He understood that to leave religious instruction to private institutions might run the risk of leaving the field open to prejudice and bigotry. On the other hand, if national education remains devoid of religious studies, there would be no way of ensuring inculcation of moral values or moulding of character on humanistic lines.

As he viewed, "It is obvious that millions of Indians are not prepared to see that their children are brought up in an irreligious atmosphere and, I am sure, you too will agree with them. What will be the consequence, if the government undertakes to impart purely secular education? Naturally people will try to provide religious education to their children through private sources. How these private sources are working today or are likely to work in future is already known to you. I know something about it and can say that not only in villages but even in cities the imparting of religious education is entrusted to teachers who though literate are not educated. To them religion means nothing but bigotry The method of education, too, is such in which there is no scope for not being able to drive out the ideas infused into them, in their early stage. If we want to safeguard the intellectual life of our country against this danger it becomes all the more necessary for us not to leave the imparting of early religious education to private sources. We should rather take it under our direct care and supervision."[13]

Bridge Between East and West

If Azad's understanding of religion flowered in humanism as the major strand of his democratic ethos, his accommodative attitude towards the cultures of both East and West, generated an atmosphere of freedom in which educational course was to follow. Apart from its significance in the political context, the principle of freedom bears closely on the unfettered growth of the intellect.

K.G. Saiyidain thus evaluated Maulana Azad's role in restructuring the cultural scene in post-independence India: "I visualize him in the words of Pundit Nehru, as a 'bridge' between the cultures of the East and the West as the man who magnificently spanned in his person the gulf between the past and the future."[14]

Azad himself stated, "In both the East and the West the prevalent systems of education have given rise to various paradoxes. In the East, we find a disproportionate emphasis on individual salvation. Man sought knowledge as a means to his own redemption has at times paid inadequate attention to social welfare and progress. In the West, on the contrary there has been a greater emphasis on the need for social progress. In fact considerations of social welfare have at limes led to the growth of totalitarian societies in which the individual has been suppressed. Today when East and West have been brought to each other through operations of science, it is necessary that the bias whether in favour of the individual or of society should be rectified and a system of education evolved which will give due regard to both individual and social values."[15]

In that same speech he viewed that the Eastern concept of education, which has looked upon it as an end, shows a truer understanding of its real nature than the Western concept, which looked upon education as a means to social welfare. In fact his perception of education as an end, his efforts to make a synthesis in giving due regards to both individual and social values stem from his concept of man. Azad viewed man as definitely superior to other earthly creatures as not only created in the image of God and 'potentially imbued with the qualities which find their perfect embodiment in Him but also as His Vice-Sergeant on earth'. At the same time Azad views that although the Eastern view of man, which he himself shares, recognized man's high status, it was not able to free the mind of man from the bonds of fatalism. But the West in spite of its materialism, and its theoretical belief in determinism did not, in practice, adopt the attitude of fatalism. It made science its guide and by applying it to the social problems led the way to the creation of new and better social order.

Thus one may find that in essence Azad wanted to make a combination of both the Eastern and the Western ideas, where man, Gods 'Vice-Sergeant' will not fall prey to the cruel hands of fatalism but will ever be conscious to guide his own fate in accordance with the social well-being. However, how far education can at all solve this conflict between power conferred by science, and vision which is the gift of Religion and Philosophy, remains unsolved. In effect that hinges upon interplay of romance and realism in Azad's ideas in the sphere of education.

Azad's penetrating eyes did not see any basic difference in the philosophies of East and West, nor did he held one superior to the other. But he discovered that important differences do exist in their mental and emotional attitudes which are related to the theories and concepts of human nature provided by the respective thinkers of East and West. The great thinkers of the West Darwin, Freud and Marx, tried to discover truth in their vastly different ways. But they failed to do so. The eastern philosophers went round and round in the labyrinth of Sufism and Vedanta. They realised the heights which man could attain but they got entangled in fatalism. Azad based his educational philosophy on the principle that there should be a bridge between the East and the West and one should not accept or reject anything old or new without applying to it the test of reason.

The impress of Azad's thinking was felt in almost every field of education. Without his guidance, it is doubtful whether free India's culture and education would have remained free of distortion. Azad laid emphasis on adult education and expanded its dimension. He promoted research in eastern learning and literature and set up the three Academies to develop the fine arts. It was he who started work on the compilation of technical terms in Hindi on a large scale. It was he who resisted the emotional approach to the issue of the medium of instruction and the conflict between Hindi and non-Hindi protagonists. It was he who established the University Grants Commission and through it safeguarded the autonomy of the universities and made available larger funds for higher education. It was he who declared that women's education was more important than men's because it could create a new consciousness and a new life in the whole nation.

Much had been said for and against the need of religious education, but none could be more aware of its need and importance than Maulana Azad. However, in the context of the conditions prevailing in the country and for certain other considerations, he decided that it would not be wise to impart religious instruction officially in government schools. At the same time he realised that the true spirit of religion should permeate not only education but every sphere of life and through it people should learn tolerance and broadmindedness and develop a strong bond of sympathy for fellow human beings.

The underlying objectives of Azad's life were to spread communal unity and to provide proper education and training for Indies welfare. He set about promoting a balanced outlook among the Indians and to fill their hearts with love and tolerance for each other. In this context, his achievement has had few parallels in the Indian history.

Azad set up the following boards/commissions during his tenure:

1. The University Education Commission (Set up 1948, Report 1949).
2. The Secondary Education Commission (Set up 1952, Report 1953).
3. All India Council for Technical Education (Reorganised to set up a chain of national laboratories throughout the country).
4. Kharagpur Institute of Higher Technology.
5. University Grants Commission.

Maulana Azad had the foresight to perceive that technical education was essential for India's progress and development. Addressing the Central Advisory Board of Education on February 6, 1958, he said (in what proved to be his last speech) :

"When I assumed charge of Education in 1947, immediately saw that there could be no solution of our educational problems without the fullest cooperation of the Centre and the Provinces. Education was no doubt a provincial subject but it was my considered opinion that this distinction could be maintained only when our educational targets have been achieved. Till such time, the Central Government should openly recognise that though education is a State subject, it must share this responsibility with the State Governments if we are to meet the challenge of the times."[16] When Azad took over the Education portfolio its budget was of only two crore rupees. Gradually he succeeded in having it increased to more than Rs. 30 crores. Azad held that the objective of Our Five Year Plans was not only to increase agricultural and industrial production, power, transport, communications etc., but to provide a proper mental climate and requisite training for the people in general and the Younger generation in particular in order to produce better citizens. No amount of material progress would be of any earthly use, he felt, if we lagged behind in education. Azad held that there was no dearth of talent, scientific or otherwise, in India, and it only needed proper encouragement and cultivation. He was, in a way, preoccupied with scientific and technical education. His broad vision however is reflected in the speech he gave in 1950 at the meeting of the Central Advisory Board of Education. He indicated that with a view to raising the standards of technical education it was proposed that in addition to the expansion and development of existing institutions, four institutes of higher technology should be set up. The Eastern Higher Technological Institute near Calcutta was being expanded although it had not even its own building till then.

On October 19, 1945, the government accepted in principle the Sargent Report which had recommended that a National Council of Technical Education be set up for development of technical education. The Council was set up as an Advisory Board on November 30, 1945 under the Chairmanship of N.R. Sarkar. In 1953, the Constitution of this Council was amended and the Minister of Education was made its President. On February 8, 1953, while assuming the Presidentship of the Council, Maulana Azad said:

"As Minister of Education I have naturally been interested in its (the Council's) working and I am happy, my association with the Council will henceforth be much closer than it has been in the past. Some of the landmarks in the history of the Council naturally come to my mind on this occasion. You are aware that it was primarily at the initiative of the Council that the Government of India decided to strengthen a number of undergraduate institutions in various parts of the country by providing grants amounting to about one and a half crores of rupees. It was also on the recommendation of the Council that the Government accepted the proposals of the Sarkar Committee to set up four higher institutes of technology in the country. The Council is also responsible for undertaking steps to establish closer relations between industries and educational institutions by establishing different types of industrial training schemes."[17]

Maulana Azad was willing to extend help for development of technical training in every possible way, whether it be for expansion of existing building, acquisition of equipment or recruitment of teachers trained in the new methods of education. He acquired, through the courtesy of the West Bengal Government, a plot of 1200 acres in Hooghly near Calcutta for setting up the Eastern Higher Technological Institute. The plot contained a collectorate building and some other houses where political prisoners were detained in the pre-independence days. Soon, however, these houses were replaced by teachers' quarters and lecture halls. Inaugurating the Kharagpur Institute of Technology on August 18, 1951 Azad said:

"One of the first decisions I took on assuming charge was that we must so improve the facilities for higher technical education in the country that we could ourselves meet most of our needs. The large number of our youngmen who had been going abroad for higher training could have received such training in the country itself. Indeed, I looked and still look forward to the day when the facilities for technical education in India will be of such a level that people from abroad will come to India for higher scientific and technical training."[18]

The Kharagpur Institute was one of Azad's achievements. In July 1955 when the first batch of hundreds of successful students passed through its gate, each of them had already received many offers of employment. This proved how accurate Azad was in assessing the country's needs.

Not content with this, Maulana Azad set up a Committee in 1947, under Sir Shanti Swarup Bhatnagar, to assess the country's requirements of scientific and technical workers for the next ten years and to recommend measures too provide them.

In the domain of fine arts, Maulana Azad was particularly fond of poetry and was himself a poet, but he was also a connoisseur of music and painting. It was, therefore, natural that he set up the three academies—Sahitya Akademi, Lalit Kala Akademi and Sangeet Natak Akademi.

These Akademies, run by separate Councils, are fully financed by the Government. The senior-most amongst them, the Sahitya

Akademi, was inaugurated on March 12, 1954. Its aim is to promote Indian literature and eminent men of letters are on its Executive Council. There are separate Boards for the main languages and, to patronise and encourage writers, the Akademi gives annual awards of Rs. 5000 for the best book in each language.

The Sangeet Natak Akademi promotes Hindustani and Karnatak music by honouring deserving vocalists and instrumentalists with Presidential awards and honours. The maestros in dance and drama are also awarded in similar manner.

The Lalit Kala Akademi concerns itself with the promotion and development of paintings, sculptures and allied arts.

Under the guidance of Maulana Azad, India became one of the founder-members of UNESCO. Inaugurating the Indian National Commission for UNESCO on April 9, 1949, Maulana Azad said that UNESCO fulfilled a great need and had done remarkably well since it was founded three years ago. India, on her part, had cooperated with UNESCO in an admirable manner and many UNESCO projects were underway in India. Classics from various countries of the world were being translated into Indian languages. The scope of exchange of scientific information and cooperation had been widened. A large number of Indian professors and scholars were holding high posts in UNESCO and India could be proud of the fact that Dr. Radhakrishnan had been elected President of the Executive Council of UNESCO.

In June 1951, speaking at the Paris session of UNESCO, Maulana Azad gave an inspiring address. His main emphasis was that UNESCO could succeed in promoting a willingness among various countries to understand each other's culture with a view to creating harmony and accord, it would be a great achievement because cultural accord would naturally lead to, accord on political and economic levels. On January 8, 1954, addressing the Indian National Commission for Cooperation with UNESCO, Maulana Azad ventilated the grievance of the eastern countries that UNESCO and its institutions were not paying due attention to them. At the same time, Maulana Azad declared in another speech, the UNESCO provided a ray of hope for peace and amity in this world.

The printed speeches of Maulana Azad are not his political or religious addresses They are mostly those speeches that he delivered as Minister of Education. Even so they cover a wide range of subject such as history, music, dance, drama, education, technical education, public schools, UNESCO, the concept of man in the East and the West, roads and progress, science, Indian literature, and many others.

Yet another achievement of Maulana Azad was the setting up of the Indian Council for Cultural Relations with the object of establishing and improving cultural relations with other countries. The Council publishes an Arabic quarterly called *Thaqafat-ul-Hind,* and its first editor was Maulana Abdur Razzak Malihabadi. This journal was issued with a view to make the West Asian countries conscious of India's culture and civilization. Another journal called the *Indo-Asia* is published in English and is circulated in those Asian countries where English is understood. It has the same object as *Thaqafat-ul-Hind.* The Council also distributes a large number of books in other countries with a view to introducing the people of those countries to Indian culture, civilization and literature.

Maulana Azad served the country in various capacities. Besides being the Education Minister, he was the Deputy Leader of the Congress Party in Parliament and a principal adviser to the Prime Minister. There is no doubt that the name of this honoured writer, politician and thinker will never lose its lustre in Indian history.

In an article K.G. Saiyidain, published in the *Education Quarterly* and reproduced in the book on Maulana Azad released by the Publications Division wrote:

"Maulana was first and last an educationist. The secret of his success as an educationist lay in the fact that he practised in his life what he preached in his works. He had the qualities of character and intellect which he wished to inculcate in the people of his country. His whole life bore a shining stamp of sincerity and truth—truth which he loved and advocated with Socratic passion; truth which makes no compromise with expediency and no concessions to ill-informed criticism or opposition, however bitter it might be....

"As a Minister, who presided over the educational destinies of the country since the attainment of independence, he has left the impress of his great personality in many directions.

"His humanism could not reconcile itself to the fact that many groups and classes should be debarred from the participation in the growing life of the country, because centuries of social neglect and tyranny had deprived them of their human rights. In order to equalise and democratize opportunity, several schemes of scholarship were initiated of which the most noticeable was one for Scheduled Castes, Scheduled Tribes and other Backward Classes for which the financial provision was raised from Rs. 300,000 to Rs. 20 million during his regime.

"Through the growing relationship with UNESCO in the cause of peace and international understanding and through the promotion of cultural exchanges with many foreign countries, cultural activities received a new stimulus in the country and Indian culture a new recognition and respect abroad. As a writer and a man of culture, he was sensitive to the financial plight of writers, artists and others working in the field of culture and he sponsored a scheme under which those in really indigent circumstances could be given financial assistance.

"He had a phased programme formulated for the development of Hindi but insisted that it should be so implemented as to give no cause for grievance or apprehension to other national languages, which were equally dear to him. When, in the first flush of freedom and nationalism, many who had themselves received western education wanted to oust English or at least relegate it to the background, this man of vision, who was himself a product of the traditional system of eastern education, insisted that English should be retained and given an important place in our national life.

"He was, above all, deeply interested in the welfare of the teacher community and worked hard not only to improve their financial condition but also to raise their social status...

"I recall with poignant interest the words that he spoke at the last meeting of the Central Advisory Board of Education only a fortnight before his death :

'Whatever may be the system that we may adopt, there can be no real improvement without an improvement in the quality of our teachers. One of the main achievements in the Second Five-Year

Plan has been the improvement of salary scales of teachers in the Primary and Basic schools...

'While these measures have gone a good deal to raise the morale of teachers, some of the good effects have been lost because of constant and carping criticisms of our existing teachers. I know that many of them are ill-trained and some have come to the profession only as a last resort, but at the same time we must recognise that in spite of great difficulties they have served the nation well...'

"But as a man, the Maulana was even greater than his work as a Minister. With what grace and dignity and sense of justice did he preside over our activities! Never interfering in details, not even greatly interested in them, unless they impinged in someway on principles or policy; always ready to help and encourage, always willing to overlook faults and weaknesses except when they encroached in anyway of the public interest or the integrity of administration; always shunning personal publicity, sometimes even with indignation. He would not even accept honorary degrees from the universities. If I remember a right, he had only once accepted such a degree in the early years of his ministership.

"The same sympathy and understanding and absence of a doctrinaire approach which enabled him to deal with complex political situations guided him in the educational field and kept the keel of our educational ship steady."[19]

It also redounds to Azad's foresight and credit that he always appointed one educationist as Secretary in the Ministry of Education, Accordingly, as long as he remained Minister of Education, his Secretaries were eminent educationists like Tara Chand, Humayun Kabir and K.G. Saiyidain.

REFERENCES

1. Weber,.Max, "The Chinese Literate" in Gerth H.H. and C. Wright Mills (eds.) *From Max Weber Essays in Sociology* (London: Routledge), 1991, p. 426.
2. Brass, Paul R., *The Politics of India Since Independence* (Cambridge: Cambridge University Press), 1994, p. 10.

3. Rabindra Nath Bhattacharyya, "Mulana Abul Kalam Azad and the Reconstruction of National Education in India (1947-58)," in Singh, Mahavir (ed.), *Maluana Abul Kalam Azad: Profile of a Nationalist, op. cit.*, p. 119.
4. *Ibid.*
5. *The Constituent Assembly Debates*, Vol. III, 1949, p. 1556.
6. Saiyidain, K.G., *Maluana Azad's Contribution to Education* (Baroda: The Maharaja Sayajirao University), 1961.
7. Address to the State Education Ministers Conference, New Delhi, September 20, 1957.
8. Opening Address at the All India Educational Conference, New Delhi, January 16, 1948.
9. Rabindra Nath Bhattacharyya, "Mulana Abul Kalam Azad and the Reconstruction of National Education in India (1947-58)," in Singh, Mahavir (ed.), *Mulana Abul Kalam Azad: Profile of a Nationalist, op. cit.*, p. 122.
10. *Ibid.*
11. *Ibid.*, p. 123.
12. *Ibid.*
13. *Presidential Address at the Fourteenth Session of the Central Advisory Board of Education*, New Delhi, January 13, 1948.
14. Saiyidain, K.G., *Maluana Azad's Contribution to Education, op. cit.*
15. Inaugural Address at the Symposium on the Concept of Man and the Philosophy of Education in the East and the West, New Delhi, December 13, 1951.
16. Address at the Central Advisory Board of Education, New Delhi, February 6, 1958.
17. Malsaini Arsh, *Abul Kalam Azad, op. cit.*, p. 84.
18. *Ibid.*, pp. 84-85.
19. *Ibid.*, pp. 88-90.

6

AZAD AND PARTITION

Maulana Azad, as he asserted in his 1923 address at Congress session, had dreamt of the edifice of India's national independence on the foundation of communal unity. It was a tragedy that the dawn of independence appeared in the midst of an orgy of communal bloodshed and partition of the country. All his efforts to avert this tragic finale to the glorious struggle had failed. Speaking on the resolution on the partition proposal when it was put before the All India Congress Committee, he said, "The partition of India is a tragedy...We tried our best to avert it but failed."

However, he was not prepared to accept it as acceptance of Two-Nation theory and pointed out:

"Yet, we should not forget that nation is one, its cultural life is one and indivisible. We have failed politically. That is why we are accepting partition. We should accept our defeat and, at the same time, try to remain confident so that our culture is not divided. If we put a stick into water, it would appear that water has been divided whereas in fact water remains one and the division disappears the moment stick is removed."[1]

For his own failure he blamed the Muslim community inasmuch as, instead of following his lead, opposed him at crucial moments. Addressing a gathering in the vicinity of Delhi's Jama Masjid, in October 1947, he gave expression to his anguish in his majestic style:

"Today India is independent; you can see India's flag serenely flying on the ramparts of Red Fort. It is the very flag at which arrogance of power used to hurl derisive laughter...Today I want to give candid expression to my feelings. The partition of united India was basically wrong. The manner, in which religious differences were widened, inevitably resulted in this tragedy that we are witnessing all over."

He himself stuck to the position he had been taking since the *Al-Hilal* days when he was calling upon the community to enthusiastically participate in the freedom struggle. Addressing a gathering of those who had decided to migrate, he said:

"This life of escape, that you are taking recourse to in the pious name of *Hijrat,* if you seriously think, you will realise that it is wrong. Strengthen your hearts and develop the habit of thinking. You will see how hasty your decision is. Where, after all are you going and why? See that the minarets of this mosque are asking you where you have lost the pages of your glorious history. Only the other day your caravans had washed their hands for prayer on the banks of Jamuna and today you are afraid of staying here."

So impressive was that speech that several of those ready to leave changed their mind and resolved to stay back. To those staying back his advice was:

"If you want that the freedom that we had dreamt about should not end in disaster and the adversity should not be allowed to enter through any door, it is our first duty to close the door through which communalism entered our life and polity. All who have eyes to see can see that there is nothing more dangerous than this and if this door is not closed a major responsibility will fall on your head. The effort that is afoot to cleanse the atmosphere will be obstructed."[2]

The effort he was referring to was the Herculean efforts of Mahatma Gandhi on the mass level and those of Nehru in administration to douche the flames of communal strife. He himself continued to work for building free India's national life in which people could develop a modern scientific outlook which alone could help them appreciate the concepts of common nationhood and common shared culture. He understood the difficulties that Muslim community was likely to face after partition but, instead of punishing them for their failure to listen to his advice, he adopted positive approach to save them from despair and develop a ghetto mentality.

To understand the extent of Azad's efforts during this period, and hence his profound sense of defeat when partition took place, one must look into the volumes on the transfer of power published by the British government. These, coupled with Wavell's testimony and several recent works that have mined this extensive documentary lode, give more details concerning Azad's role than does his own account in *India Wins Freedom.* Azad and his Congress colleagues were released from prison in June 1945, and soon thereafter the Viceroy assembled a conference of Indian political leaders at Simla to discuss the formation of a provisional or interim government.[4] The war with Japan was still on, and the British government was still headed by that tenacious imperialist, Winston Churchill. The Congress leaders had been out of circulation for three years and during that time a great deal had happened. For one thin Jinnah, who stayed out of jail, had been building up support for the idea of Pakistan. For another, Field-Marshal Lord Wavell who had been Commander-in-Chief, was now Viceroy. The war, which in 1942 had looked bleak for Britain and its allies was now almost over, and thus it was time to start thinking, about future political arrangements. Change was in the air, but none of the principals assembled at Simla knew the government would soon take over in Britain, that the Japan would end with the atomic cataclysms of August, and that elections in India, and even independence, were not as far off as they imagined.

The Congress leaders had every reason to be mistrustful of British intentions, for the Viceroy's proposals resembled closely the Cripps offer of 1942. At that time, Sir Stafford Cripps, a Labour member of the war cabinet, had come to India with a power-sharing offer in the interests of rallying Indian support for the war effort. Congress ultimately rejected his offer for a provisional national government as a 'post-dated cheque on a failing bank' (Gandhi's approximate phrase). But the Cripps mission failed because the Viceroy, Wavell's stubborn predecessor Lord Linlithgow, and Churchill, the Prime Minister, undercut Cripps by their unwillingness to grant Indian desires for real, as opposed to potential, authority.[5] The Congress then launched the Quit India movement and its leaders were imprisoned. Consequently, when Wavell put forward a Cripps like proposal at Simla in 1945, it was reasonable for the Congress leaders to treat it with some skepticism. The context for the offer had changed, however, how greatly, Azad and his Congress colleagues did not perhaps realize. This Viceroy was sincere in his desire to work with a representative Indian Central Government. The British electorate, faced with the need to rebuild at home after the war, was turning against imperial involvement, Churchill to the contrary notwithstanding.

The major issue was the composition of the interim government. Azad, speaking for the Congress, emphasized its national, non-communal character. In other words, Congress would not accept the limitation of its nominees to caste Hindus, for that would place Congress in the position of being a communal organization. Jinnah, on the other hand, maintained the exclusive right of the Muslim League to nominate all Muslim members of the interim government and would not accept that Congress might name a nationalist Muslim (such as Azad). The issue was one of principle, but the animus was personal as well. Jinnah refused to meet Azad as a representative of the Congress, prompting Wavell to comment on Jinnah's abysmal manners. Azad was deeply hurt. Jinnah also demanded parity between the League and the Congress in the number of members each party could nominate. The Congress delegates thought this was out of line, but Wavell was prepared to accept parity between caste Hindus and Muslims (if not between the Congress and the League).[6] After days of haggling, adjournment for private discussions, and more haggling, Wavell proposed an interim government composed of five caste Hindus (three Congress and two non-Congress, five Muslims (four League and one Punjab Unionist), one Sikh, two scheduled-caste members, and one Indian Christian. Jinnah adamantly refused to accept a non-League Muslim, and thus Wavell concluded the proceedings, taking the blame upon himself for the failure of the conference. Azad was impressed by Wavell's sincerity and impartiality, and in his statement at the end of the conference placed the blame for its failure squarely on the Muslim League and Jinnah's intransigence. Wavell was inclined to agree, but also recognized the basis for Jinnah's intransigence: Muslim fears of Congress domination.

Though Jinnah and the Muslim League may fairly be blamed for the failure of the Simla conference, the Congress attitude did not give Jinnah any reason to change his position. Congress claimed to be the only truly national party, dismiss Muslim League's claim to be the sole representative of Muslims and refused to recognize Muslim fears of majority domination. The Congress command tended to regard the League as same party that they had whipped decisively in the elections 1937, at which point they had demanded, as the price of coalition with the League, that League members join the Congress and submit to party direction. Jinnah regarded that as tantamount to his party's suicide and refused, and since that time had build up a substantial—if still fragile-base of support. At Simla Jinnah once again drew the line at a concession that he regarded as 'abject surrender' and 'a death knell to the Muslim League'.[7] Azad, however, still looked upon the League as a party of self-interested individuals who marched to the government's tune, not nationalists at all.[8]

The Simla conference had no sooner concluded than Churchill's government was voted out of office and Attlee's Labour government came to power, the war ended abruptly, and provincial elections were held in India in late 1945 and early 1946. The Congress won in its areas of dominance, but so too did the Muslim League, particularly in the provinces that Jinnah claimed for Pakistan. So both parties had a renewed justification for their claims to represent either the Indian nation as a whole or the Muslim nation. Azad remained President of the Congress throughout this period, and the documentary evidence suggests that he tried to bring about a shift in the Congress position towards some acknowledgment of the seriousness of Muslim fears, and of the need to make some concessions in order to avoid the vivisection of the subcontinent.

Shortly after the collapse of the Simla conference, for example, Azad wrote to Mahatma Gandhi that the Muslims were afraid and their fears could be removed only by devising a plan under which they would feel secure. He proposed the following: (a) a federal constitution for India with fully autonomous provincial units; the centre would control only those subjects of an all India nature that the constituent units had agreed to; (b) the units would have the right of secession; (c) there would be joint electorates at the centre and in the provinces, but with reservation of seats; (d) parity of Hindus and Muslims in the central legislature and the central executive; (e) a convention whereby the head of the Indian federation would be Hindu and Muslim by turn. Azad argued against the Congress long-held position that a strong centre was essential for Indian unity. He appealed to his Hindu colleagues to leave entirely to Muslims the decision concerning their status in the future constitution of India. If Muslims were convinced that this decision was not being imposed upon them by non-Muslims, he argued, they would drop all talk of partition and realize that their best interests lay with a federated and united India.

Azad was doubtless overly sanguine about Muslim, or at least the Muslim League, response to his plan. Nevertheless, by calling for a decentralized federation and for Hindu-Muslim parity in the central government and legislature, he conceded two major points that the Congress later accepted during the Cabinet Mission negotiations in 1946. Gandhi responded to Azad's heartfelt proposals:

"I do not infer from your letter that you are writing about my Hindus. Whatever you have in your heart has not appeared in your writing. But don't worry, we will talk the matter over when we meet, if you so desire. Whatever you want to say about the communal problems should not be said without consulting the Working Committee. I also am of the opinion that it would be better to keep quiet. The party can give its opinion after consultations with you.... I do not feel urge to do anything hastily."[9]

The government official who intercepted this correspondence noted laconically: 'This is not very encouraging for Azad.'

Azad recognized the need to compromise with the League in order to avoid partition. The election campaigns in late 1945 and early 1946, however, only exacerbated the differences between Congress and the Muslim League and made compromise more difficult. Sources both within the British official and without noted that partition might be inevitable. After the Muslim League's successes in the provincial elections, Jinnah was in a strong position to resist any agreement. Mentioning, Azad as the only Muslim of national importance still in the Congress, one commentator noted, unkindly: 'The Congress' claim to represent more than the Hindus rests on very slight foundations.' Indian leaders, meanwhile, were increasingly sceptical of the government's intention, or ability, to do anything to solve the communal deadlock.[10]

Azad in this period wrote to and met the Viceroy several times and urged him and, through him, the Labour government to create an atmosphere for peaceful change. In his speeches he also urged the people to avoid clashes:

"India is passing through the birth-pangs of freedom on the one hand, and the ordeal of many privations ... which always form part of the aftermath of a war on the other. The natural urge of freedom accentuated by the past five years of war has given poignancy to the impatience of every sector of the population in India.... The situation does not admit of over-simplified formulas of action. It is difficult and complex and demands the most careful and cautious handling. I must, therefore, appeal to all the parties in the country to exercise restraint and allow the situation to be confined to manageable proportions."[11]

The Labour government, in response to pressures at home and in India to find a way out of the communal tangle that would lead to Indian independence, sent the Cabinet Mission to India in the spring of 1946. The Secretary of State for India, Lord Pethick-Lawrence, was accompanied by Sir Stafford Cripps and A.V. Alexander—the 'Magi', as Wavell called them but these three men, in the end, were not wise enough to devise a workable plan.[12]

Azad met the members of the mission on 3 April and presented the Congress position, based upon notes by Nehru, with Sardar Patel's concurrence. The Congress position, as Azad presented it, resembled his own scheme of the previous August in one major respect: the Congress backed the idea of a federation of autonomous provinces with residuary powers vested in the provinces. This plan envisaged two lists of subjects: compulsory and optional. Any given province would have three choices: to stand out of the constitution, to federate for compulsory subjects only, or to federate for both compulsory and optional subjects. The Congress also insisted that the negotiations had to proceed on the basis of a grant of Indian independence, that an interim government should be formed even before the constitution-making body was called, and finally, that the composition of that interim government be on the basis of provincial representation-parity for Muslims was not mentioned, although some minority representation was.

After presenting the Congress position, Azad went on to make some personal observations. He felt that those Muslims who backed the idea of Pakistan did meant. It would be injurious to Muslim interests. Many Muslis\ms would inevitably be left in India and would be treated as aliens. Therefore, he said, there must be a federal government so that all Muslims can pull their weight together. When asked about the status of Hindu and Sikh minorities left in what might become Pakistan, Azad replied that such minorities would be relatively more numerous, powerful, and better educated than the Muslims left in India, and thus better able to protect themselves. The Secretary of State was non-plussed by this idea of aliens on either side of the border; Cripps said it was 'juridically impossible', and Wavell felt that Azad had raised this 'novel theory' as a debating point against Jinnah's theory of Muslims as a separate nationality. Though his British interlocutors deprecated this idea, Azad was voicing real Muslim fears. He did not use the more ominous term 'hostages', although League leaders certainly did.[13]

When asked what would be the Congress reaction to a sub-federal grouping of particular provinces, Azad stated that though the Congress had agreed to provincial autonomy (a major concession), it could not agree to any form of partition. Congress might consider a proposal for grouping, but there were limits to how far it would go. Having lobbied for provincial autonomy, he knew those limits only too well. Further, when asked about parity for Muslims in the central government, Azad said Congress had not considered this, but he would try to promote it.[14]

Azad did a lot of personal lobbying, both with the Cabinet Mission and with his colleagues in the Congress, during the hot months of 1946. In April, he made two private and unauthorized interventions in the negotiating process, approaching the Cabinet Mission first to ascertain their likely offer to Jinnah, in order to feel out the Congress reaction; and secondly, venturing the view that he might be able to get Congress to agree to some form of grouping of provinces for optional subjects. Azad was handicapped because he could not see the third party in the drama—Jinnah still refused to meet with him as a Muslim representative of Congress and would agree to meet only a Hindu Congressman. Azad was also handicapped by Mahatma Gandhi. From their exchange of correspondence of the previous August, it was clear that the Mahatma was unwilling to go as far as Azad in meeting Muslim fears and Muslim League demands. Now, again, Gandhi was shocked at Azad's informal initiatives *vis-a-vis* the mission.[15]

The Cabinet Mission decided to call together delegates from the Congress and the Muslim League to thrash out their differences away from the heat of Delhi, apparently at Azad's suggestion.[16] In early May, accordingly, four Congressmen, four Leaguers, the Viceroy, and the "Magi" convened in Simla. The omens were not good. In accepting the invitation for the Congress, Azad revealed that Congress still refused to consider the grouping of provinces on a communal basis. Gandhi in particular was against this idea. When the conference opened, Jinnah refused to shake Azad's proffered hand, to the Maulana's visible annoyance. Further, on the second day of the conference, Azad sent a letter to the Secretary of State declaring that Congress would accept neither provincial grouping, nor parity of different communal groups in the central executive legislature. Azad, in other words, had been unable to persuade his Congress colleagues to move towards compromise with the League. Even though Nehru, apparently, was 'co-operative', neither Azad's plan of the previous August nor the hopes he voiced privately to the mission had been accepted by the Congress committee. This Simla conference, like the one a year earlier, ended without agreement.

The Cabinet Mission Plan, announced on 16 May, incorporated a complex, three-tiered governmental scheme that involved provincial grouping. Also included in the plan were procedures for establishing a constitution-making body and an interim government. The mission hoped that the League would accept a plan that grouped the Muslim provinces but stopped short partition, and that, with Nehru and Azad lobbying for it, Congress would accept the plan in spite of grouping, since it offered a way to hold India together. The initial reaction from the Congress was equivocal. Azad, in his official Congress letter, asked for assurances that the interim government would have the same powers as that of a cabinet in an independent dominion. But then, in a friendlier personal letter to Wavell, he noted that the Viceroy's assurance on this score was all that was necessary. Further, he said, the composition of the cabinet would not present a problem. Azad had already announced his decision to step down as President of the Congress, and as his later action makes clear, was prepared to stay out of the cabinet so that Jinnah's objection to a Congress Muslim would not wreck the chances of forming an interim government.[17]

Both the Congress, with some reservations, and the Muslim. League accepted the Cabinet Mission's statement of 16 May as a basis on which to proceed. By mid-June the Viceroy and the three wise men believed that they were on the verge of securing an agreement between the parties on the formation of an interim government. Then disaster struck. Azad, as the chief Congress Muslim, may have been willing to stay out of the interim government, but Gandhi stubbornly maintained the principle that Congress represented all communities in India. The Congress committee therefore voted against coming into the interim government in the face of Jinnah's insistence that the Muslim League have the right to name all Muslim members of the government. Wavell fumed about Gandhi's being the "real wrecker", about Jinnah's being "too uncompromising on the non-League Muslim issue", and he complimented Azad for being "honest, moderate, and a gentleman". The Viceroy was depressed about future prospects, the Cabinet Mission went home.[18]

When Azad relinquished the Congress presidency to Nehru in July 1946, and Nehru held his press conference that Azad characterized as "one of those unfortunate events which changed the course of history", things went from bad to worse. Azad, in his autobiography, seems to have regretted giving up his command at that juncture, but to explain the hardening of the Congress position solely in terms of the change of personnel is entirely too simple. The fact is that attempts to bring about an agreement between Congress and the Muslim League in the context of the Cabinet Mission's very complex proposals had foundered by the end of

June 1946. They had failed in spite of Azad's best efforts and, given Jinnah's refusal to deal with him as a Congress spokesman, Azad doubtless felt at the time that his continuation in office would impede further negotiations. Then too, although Nehru's statement at his press conference that Congress would enter the constituent assembly "unfettered by agreement" was rash, his reflection that the Cabinet Mission's plan for grouping would not work was quite realistic.[19]

Azad continued to work behind the scenes in the months ahead to bring about an agreement based on the Cabinet Mission's proposals as the only hope of avoiding partition. It was a very slim hope. He stayed out of the interim government when it was first formed, although Congress insisted on its right to name a nationalist Muslim as part of its contingent when the Muslim League came into the coalition in October 1946. He was not, therefore, party to the London talks in December 1946, yet another last-ditch attempt to forge a Congress-League agreement. Azad finally joined the interim government in January 1947, thus beginning his long career as Education Minister. By that time, Wavell was about to be replaced as Viceroy, and the pendulum of official opinion was swinging inexorably towards the view that partition was the only way out of an increasingly sticky situation.

In his search for the "Guilty Men of 1947", Maulana Abul Kalam Azad fixes upon two persons. On page 198 of the unexpurgated edition of his book *India Wins Freedom* published in 1988, he says: "It would not perhaps be unfair to say that Vallabhbhai Patel was the founder of Indian partition."[20]

According to Maulana Azad, even Sardar Patel "threw his weight in favour of partition out of irritation and injured vanity. He found himself frustrated at every step by the veto put on his proposals by Liaquat Ali Khan as Finance Minister (in the Interim Government). It was therefore in sheer anger that he decided that, if there was no other alternative, partition should be accepted."[21]

Sardar Patel was also convinced that the new state of Pakistan was not viable and could not last. He thought that the acceptance of Pakistan would teach the Muslim League a bitter lesson. Pakistan would collapse in a short time and the provinces which had seceded from India would have to face untold difficulty and hardship. Sardar Patel also said that he was now convinced that Muslims and Hindus could not be united into one nation. There was no alternative except to recognise the fact. This way alone could solve the quarrel between Hindus and Muslims. He further said that "if two brothers cannot stay together, they divide. After separation with their respective shares, they become friends. If, on the other hand, they are forced to stay together they tend to fight everyday. It was better to have one clean fight and then separate then have bickerings everyday."[22]

Patel was convinced that he could not work with the Muslim League. He openly said that he was prepared to let the League have a part of India if only he could get rid of it.

The second person whom Azad blames for the partition of the country in 1947 is Jawaharlal Nehru. He accuses Nehru of committing two serious "blunders" which led to the partition of the country: two "unfortunate events which changed the course of history", "the two greatest tragedies of Indian history".[23]

The first event relates to mid-1937—the parleys between the leaders of the Congress and those of the Muslim League in the United Provinces for a possible coalition ministry after the 1937 provincial elections. Azad's simplistic version on pages 170-72 of the revised/enlarged edition (and on pages 143-45 of the first/ expurgated edition) of his memoirs runs somewhat like this: Nehru, who, according to Azad, had first agreed in the summer of 1937 to the inclusion of two Muslim Leaguers—Chaudhari Khaliquzzaman and Nawab Muhammad Ismail Khan—in the proposed Congress ministry in the United Provinces under Govind Ballabh Pant, later, presumably under the influence of Purushottam Das Tandon, and without consulting him (Azad), informed the two League leaders that only one of them could be included. This was unacceptable to the League leaders and the negotiations between the parties broke down. "This was", he says, "a most unfortunate development. If the League's offer of cooperation had been accepted, the Muslim League party would have for all practical purposes merged in the Congress. Jawaharlal's action gave the Muslim League in the UP a new lease of life. All students of Indian politics know that it was from the U.P. that the League was re-organized. Jinnah took full advantage of the situation and started an offensive which ultimately led to Pakistan.'[24]

But the charge can easily be rebutted. Nehru was not particularly keen for the Congress forming ministries, and the issue of "office acceptance" by the Congress was not settled until early July 1937. He did not play a key role in Congress affairs in the UP at this time. Azad has not produced any evidence to substantiate his charge. Neither at that time not even later during his life he ever accused Nehru of this great lapse in public. Khaliquzzaman—who played a prominent role in the parleys in the UP in mid-1937—never accused Nehru of this "blunder".[25] Nehru's own version of the episode contained in a contemporary communication-letter to Rajendra Prasad, dated 21 July 1937[26]—which is a far more reliable piece of evidence than any recollection or reconstruction it so many decades later—is contrary to what Azad has—or is reported to have alleged. No communication of Nehru saying that only one Muslim Leaguer would be taken in the ministry and not two has ever been produced.

Now Azad's second charge against Nehru. He says that by making that "unfortunate statement" at a press conference in Bombay on 10 July 1946—that the Congress would enter the Constituent Assembly completely unfettered, 'free to modify the Cabinet Mission Plan...(Nehru) reopened the whole question of political and communal settlement...(and) Jinnah took full advantage of his mistake and withdrew from the League's early acceptance of 'the Cabinet Mission Plan'. Azad calls it "one of the greatest tragedies of Indian history".[27] Surprisingly enough, Azad refers to the press conference in Bombay, on 10 July 1946, but seems to "have forgotten about the AIUC session three days ago in the same place, when Nehru had remarked, "We are not bound by a single thing except that we have decided to go to the Constituent Assembly.'[28] After all, what Nehru was doing at the press conference on 10 July was to clarify his previous statement at the AICC session on 7 July Nehru was not rejecting the framework of the Cabinet Mission Plan. What he was doing was to make clear that the Congress had accepted that Plan putting its own construction on its most controversial part, namely, the grouping of provinces.

The Congress had accepted the Mission Plan saying that it did not regard grouping as being compulsory; while the League had accepted it saying that it regarded grouping as compulsory. So before we deal with Azad's accusation, let us be clear what the controversy was about.

By the time the Cabinet Mission came out to India in 1946 the British had decided to divide and quit the country. They feared that there was going to be a "bloody revolution" in India and they were anxious to evacuate as early as possible.[29] But they were also anxious that the responsibility for the partition of India should be firmly fixed on Indian shoulders. On their arrival in India, the Mission first offered Jinnah the small Pakistan which he ultimately got (and which, incidentally, Gandhi had already offered Jinnah during his talks with him in 1944), but which Jinnah refused to accept saying that he regarded it as being 'a maimed, mutilated and moth-eaten Pakistan'.[30] The Mission then tried to give Jinnah his "big" Pakistan through the backdoor. The Cripps Mission in 1942 had already given the provinces the right of secession from the Indian Union. This was now dangerous from the point of view of the Muslim League, because the North-West Frontier Province and Assam were controlled by the Congress. So the Mission allowed the right of secession both to the provinces and to the groups of provinces by a simple majority.

The Cabinet Mission did not prescribe a constitution for India. They only arranged for a machinery for framing the constitution for India in three stages/tiers: first, the constitution for India (and here it was understood that the Centre will have no other powers except those for defence, foreign affairs and communications); second, the constitutions for all the provinces, and, third, the constitutions for groups of provinces.

The most important part of the Mission Plan was the grouping of provinces. The Mission proposed to call them 'Hindustan' and 'Pakistan' provinces, but at the suggestion of V.P. Menon and B.N. Rau it was decided to call them "A", "B" and "C" groups of provinces. The "A" group included Madras, Bombay, the CP, the UP, Bihar, and Orissa. The "B" group included the NWFP, the Punjab and Sindh. The "C" group included Assam and Bengal. The plan provided that provinces or groups of provinces could leave the Union after every ten years.[31]

The proposals of the Cabinet Mission were, as Sir Stafford Cripps later admitted, deliberately kept vague in order that they might mean different things to different parties. For example, in one place it was said that provinces might form groups (this made grouping optional), but in another place it was laid down that provinces would form groups (this made grouping compulsory). The Congress accepted the proposal believing that grouping was optional, and, as it controlled Assam and the North-West Frontier Province, it felt confident that there would be no grouping. The Muslim League insisted that grouping was compulsory, and the British Government later upheld the League's interpretation. If the Congress had accepted compulsory grouping, the proposed B and C groups of provinces would have, in effect, given Jinnah and the Muslim League the "big" Pakistan which they wanted, and India would have been left with a weak minimal Centre.

The Cabinet Mission Plan was not meant to preserve the unity of India, but to give the Muslim League a "big" Pakistan through the backdoor (after ten years or even earlier if it could wrest it). This is confirmed by documents which have since become available. S.R. Mehrotra made one fact very clear that while the Mission was still in India, the then Viceroy, Lord Wavell, and his advisers prepared in late May 1946 what was called "a breakdown plan".[32] According to this plan, the British were to "hand over the Hindu provinces (Madras, Bombay, the UP, the CP, Bihar and Orissa) by agreement and as peaceably as possible to Hindu rule, withdrawing our troops and officials in an orderly manner, and at the same time support the Muslim provinces of India (the NWFP, the Punjab, Sindh, Bengal and Assam) against Hindu domination and assist them to work out their own constitution.'[33] Luckily for India, the British Prime Minister, Clement Attlee, did not approve of it.

It is surprising that Azad should maintain in his memoirs that both the Congress and the Muslim League had accepted the Cabinet Mission proposals. The Congress' acceptance was conditional: it had put its own interpretation on the grouping part. The League's acceptance was also conditional: it had construed the grouping part in its own way, and it relied on the British to help it in realizing its ambition. What is more significant is the fact that the League's acceptance was not final: the League accepted the Mission Plan "in the hope that it would ultimately result in the establishment of a completely sovereign Pakistan". As the League made no secret of its design to use the Mission Plan as a stepping-stone to Pakistan, so the Congress made no secret of its design to use the Mission Plan (and the Constituent Assembly) to preserve the unity and integrity of India. Nehru's only fault—if it can be described as a fault—was that he made known what the Congress intended to do. That it made Jinnah resile from his earlier conditional acceptance of the Mission Plan is another matter. Professor Robin Moore rightly describes the acceptance by both the Congress and the League of the Cabinet Mission Plan "the illusion of an agreement".[34]

The Cabinet Mission Plan offered the League the temptation of securing a big Pakistan, provided it was willing to try and work for some time—ten years at the most—the constitution of an Indian Union; and at the same time it offered the Congress the temptation of preserving at least the semblance of Indian unity, provided it was willing to run the risk of India being divided not only into two but three or more parts in the future. Not unnaturally, both the Congress and the League at first showed interest in the proposals of the Cabinet Mission and then shied away from them.

To understand the situation one has to recall the process that started with the confrontation between the British and the Congress on the question of war. The Congress had decided to non-cooperate with the government unless it conceded the demand for independence. This was reiterated in a resolution of the Working Committee in July 1940, in a milder form saying that Congress would support the British against fascism, provided the British government makes an immediate and unequivocal declaration to concede complete independence and set up a transitional national government at the Centre which should have the confidence of the elected members of the Constituent Assembly and of the responsible governments in the provinces.

On the other hand Jinnah had got the Muslim League to pass the Pakistan resolution in the background of assurance by the

Viceroy Lord Linlithgow that no constitutional change would be effected without his consent. He sharply criticised the Congress resolution and dissuaded Sir Sikandar Hayat Khan also from his intended efforts for compromise between Congress and Muslim League. He had also offered all help to the government in the war effort.

Maulana Azad, as Congress President, tried to convince Jinnah to change his rigid attitude and sent to him a confidential telegram:

"I have read your statement of 9 July. Delhi resolution is genuine about national government which would mean a coalition not confined to any single party. But is the League not prepared to agree to any transitional scheme which is not based on Two-Nation scheme?"

Jinnah's response to this was not only negative but positively insulting. He wrote back:

"I don't want your confidence in exchange for this (agreement). I refuse to talk to you through correspondence or any other mode because you have totally lost confidence of Muslim India. Don't you feel that the Congress has made you a show-boy President to hoodwink non-Congress parties and other countries of the world? You represent neither Muslims nor Hindus. This Congress is a Hindu organisation and, if you have any self-respect, you should resign forthwith. Whatever harms you could cause to the League you have done. You know that you have failed and therefore give up all this."[35]

It is a measure of Azad's generosity and commitment to the cause of unity that in spite of this impudence he did not oppose Gandhi's effort to persuade him. The tragedy is that with all his sincerity Gandhi could not bring about a change of heart in Jinnah. His response to Gandhi was no different. Ignoring all pleadings of Gandhi, he reasserted his Two Nation theory saying:

"We can confidently affirm that according to all standards and definitions, Muslims and Hindus are two major nations. We are a nation of ten crore people; we have separate cultures, languages and literatures, art and architecture, mode of naming, consciousness of values, ethical and legal principles, rites and rituals, calendar, history, traditions, tendencies and aspirations. In short we have a distinct style and way of life. We are a nation in terms of all international measures and principles."[36]

That Jinnah would not be amenable to any arguments should have been evident from the experience of 1936-37, when he had brazenly betrayed the promises he had made to leaders of Jamiat Ulama Hind and other nationalist organisations who had constituted a Unity Board to contest elections under the 1935 Act. Muslim League was almost a defunct organisation and could not hope to win a single seat without their help. He therefore sought the help of Unity Board for elections with the promise that he would cleanse the League of feudal elements. After the elections, when he acted contrary to this promise and admitted into League Parliamentary Board the very feudal elements who had earlier refused to contest elections as League candidates, he was reminded of his undertaking. To this had replied that 'those were political promises.' In other words he believed that political promises were not meant to be honoured.

That Jinnah was just playing a game and not serious about his theory is evident from the position he adopted in his first address to the Constituent Assembly of the newly created nation state of Pakistan. After having defeated the efforts of Azad and Gandhi, thanks to the cunning of the imperialist rulers he advocated united nationhood for the new country and advised its inhabitants not to look upon themselves in terms of Hindus and Muslims but as Pakistanis. On the basis of that one statement some historians have made out that he was really a secularist and run down Gandhi and Azad for mixing religion and politics in contravention of the secular principle of their separation.

Maulana Azad had exposed the hypocrisy of Jinnah way back in 1937 when, in support of Muslim Mass Contact campaign, launched during Nehru's presidency of Congress. The conference had issued a statement on the lines of Azad's thinking and Jinnah had questioned the purpose of the gathering. Reacting to that Azad issued the following statement:

"Mr. Jinnah has anxiously raised the question about the conference of UP Congressmen. He might be under the impression that we are betraying the Muslims. Regarding our sincerity Mr.

Jinnah should know that during the last 15 years we have participated in all the movements of Muslims.

"Has Mr. Jinnah ever tried to understand the woes of Muslims? Some of us are of the opinion that Mr. Jinnah and his associates are made of foreign material and have no concern for the common Indians.

"On the other hand Congress is preparing both Hindus and Muslims for economic and political struggle. It has a history of suffering and sacrifice in which we Muslims have made significant contributions. In the last elections it has defeated the reactionaries among Hindus whereas Mr. Jinnah has played a leading role in strengthening the reactionary elements among Muslims. Does he want Muslims to continue treading the path of reaction which means death? Our survival depends on keeping away from Mr. Jinnah and his friends who have kept Muslims away from the national struggle against imperialism."[37]

No sacrifice was too heavy if it could serve the cause. Even while presenting cogent arguments to prove that all inhabitants of India constituted one nation he had no hesitation in meeting some of the demands of Jinnah and offer safeguards for the community against his conviction that Muslims should make a common cause with Hindus, without any conditions, because struggle for freedom was their religious obligation. It may be the naivete of Azad and his Congress colleagues that they hoped to change his heart with their personal sincerity and scientific approach to nationhood.

In his recently published book *India Wins* Errors—A Scrutiny of Maulana Azad's *India Wins Freedom,* Rajmohan Gandhi has countered the Maulana's stand on the partition and has quoted the proceedings of the AICC to prove that "he (Maulana Azad) asked the AICC to vote for the resolution. Actually he seconded it." Rajmohan quotes Maulana Azad as having said that "The Cabinet Mission's Scheme was better than the partition proposal but he supported the resolution because a settlement must be reached at all costs to make the British quit at the earliest...A concession has to be made to the Muslim League's obstinacy. He had told the Viceroy that the country could brook no delay and the question should be settled either way at once. The seceding parts would hurry back to the union."[38]

Rajmohan Gandhi has also referred to the meeting of the Congress Working Committee held on 9 June 1947 where besides other leaders Maulana Azad was also present. In this meeting as Rajmohan Gandhi quotes from (File G/43 of 1947 in the AICC Papers) to authenticate this view, that Azad did not oppose the partition proposal, Acharya J. B. Kripalani has refuted the Maulana's observation that he opposed the partition.[39] Ram Manohar Lohia in his work *Guilty Men* also held the same view. Lohia writes: "Two of us socialists, Mr. Jayaprakash Narayan and I, were specially invited to this meeting. Barring us two, Mahatma Gandhi and Khan Abdul Ghaffar Khan, none spoke a single word against partition.

"Maulana Azad sat in a chair throughout this meeting in a comer of the very small room which packed us all, puffed away at his endless cigarettes and spoke not a word.

"Khan Abdul Ghaffar Khan spoke a bare two sentences. He expressed his sorrow over the fact that his colleagues had accepted the scheme of partition. As a small mercy he wanted them to find out if the proposed plebiscite in the NWFP could include the alternative of independence alongside of the two other choices of accession to India or Pakistan..."[40]

In defence of the Maulana, it can be said, that as a seasoned and sober statesman of his eminence and calibre and a great disciplinarian, he was not expected to indulge in rhetoric when he knew that the partition had already been agreed to by Gandhiji, Nehru and Patel and therefore, there was no use opposing it.

REFERENCES

1. Bhutani, Surender, *Maulana Azad and Indian Polity, op. cit.*, p. 127.
2. Speech at Jama Masjid Delhi, 1948, quoted in Malsaini Arsh, *Abul Kalam Azad, op. cit.*
3. Mansergh, Nicholas (ed.), *Transfer of Power 1942-47* (in 12 Volumes) (London: Her Majesty's Stationery Office), 1973.
4. Menon, V. P., *The Transfer of Power in India* (Princeton: Princeton University Press), 1957, p. 191.

5. Moore, R.J., *Churchill, Cripps and India 1939-45* (Oxford: Oxford University Press), 1975, pp. 114-32.
6. Menon, V.P., *The Transfer of Power in India, op. cit.*, pp. 181-215.
7. Jalal, Ayesha, *The Sole Spokesman: Jinnah, The Muslim League and The Demand for Pakistan* (Cambridge: Cambridge University Press), 1985, p. 132.
8. Azad, Maulana Abul Kalam, *India Wins Freedom, op. cit.*, pp. 110-111.
9. Douglas, Ian Henderson, *Abul Kalam Azad: An Intellectual and Religious Biography, op. cit.*, pp. 297-98.
10. *Ibid.*
11. *The Hindustan Times*, New Delhi, 3-3-1946.
12. Douglas, Ian Henderson, *Abul Kalam Azad: An Intellectual and Religious Biography, op. cit.*, p. 299.
13. Mansergh, Nicholas (ed.), *Transfer of Power 1942-47*, Volume 7, p. 46.
14. *Ibid.*
15. *Ibid.*
16. *Ibid.*
17. *Ibid.*, p. 303.
18. *Ibid.*, pp. 294-315.
19. Azad, Maulana Abul Kalam, *India Wins Freedom, op. cit.*, p. 154.
20. *Ibid.*, p. 198.
21. Chopra, P.N., *Maulana Abul Kalam Azad Unfulfilled Dreams* (New Delhi: Interprint), 1990, p. 72.
22. *Ibid.*, p. 81.
23. Azad, Maulana Abul Kalam, *India Wins Freedom, op. cit.*, pp. 164, 170.
24. *Ibid.*, p. 170.
25. Khaliquzzaman, Chaudhri, *Pathway to Pakistan* (Lahore: S.M. Ashraf), 1961, Chapters XVI, XVII.
26. Gopal, S. (ed.), *Selected Works of Jawaharlal Nehru*, Vol. 8 (New Delhi: Oxford), 1976, pp. 165-71.
27. Azad, Maulana Abul Kalam, *India Wins Freedom, op. cit.*, pp. 164-70.
28. Gopal, S. (ed.), *Selected Works of Jawaharlal Nehru*, Vol. 15, *op. cit.*, pp. 241-48.
29. Mehrotra, S.R., Towards India Freedom and Partition (Delhi: Rupa), 1979, p. 230.
30. Hudson, H.V., *The Great Divide* (London: Allen and Unwin), 1969, p. 113.
31. Mehrotra, S. R., "Mulana Abul Kalam Azad and Jawaharlal Nehru; 'Blunder' Leading to the Partition India 1947", in Singh, Mahavir (ed.), *Mulana Abul Kalam Azad: Profile of a Nationalist, op. cit.*, p. 27.
32. *Ibid.*
33. Moon, Penderal (ed.), *Wavell: The Viceroy's Journal, London*, 1973, p. 485.
34. Mehrotra, S.R., "Mulana Abul Kalam Azad and Jawaharlal Nehru; 'Blunder' Leading to the Partition India 1947", in Singh, Mahavir (ed.), *Mulana Abul Kalam Azad. Profile of a Nationalist, op. cit.*, pp. 28-29.

35. Bhutani, Surender, *Maulana Azad and Indian Polity, op. cit.*, pp. 131-32.
36. *Ibid.*
37. *Ibid.*, p. 134.
38. Gandhi, Rajmohan, *India Wins Error—A Scrutiny of Maulana Azad's India Wins Freedom* (New Delhi: Penguin), 2002.
39. Kripalani, J.B., *Gandhi: His Life and Thought* (New Delhi: Publications Division, Ministry of Information and Broadcasting, Government of India), 1970.
40. Lohia, Ram Manohar, *Guilty Men of India's Partition* (Allahabad: Kitabistan), 1960.

BIBLIOGRAPHY

Abdullah, S.M., *Spirit and Substance of Urdu Prose* (Lahore: Ashraf), 1940.

Ahmad, Aziz, *Islamic Modernism in India and Pakistan, 1857-1964* (London: Oxford University Press), 1967.

Ahmed, Sufia, *Muslim Community in Bengal, 1884-1912* (Dacca: Oxford University Press), 1974.

Albiruni, A.H., *Makers of Pakistan and Modern Muslim India* (Lahore: Ashraf), 1950.

Ahmad, Nazir, *Ibn ul Waqt* (Lahore: Sheikh Mubarak Ali), 1949.

Ahmad, Jamil-ud-Din (ed.), *Speeches and Writings of Mr. Jinnah*, Vol. I (Lahore: Ashraf), 1960.

Ahmed, Akbar S., *Jinnah, Pakistan and Islamic Identity* (Karachi: Oxford University Press).

Ahmad, Aziz, *Islamic Modernism in India and Pakistan 1857-1964* (London: Oxford University Press), 1967.

Ahmad, Rizwan (ed.) *The Quaid-e-Azam Papers* (Karachi: East & West Publishing Co.), 1976.

Ahmad, Rizwan (ed.) *Iqbal's Letters to Quaid-e-Azam* (Lahore: Friends Educational Service), 1966.

Akbar, Ahmad, *Jinnah Pakistan and Islamic Identity* (London: Routledge), 1997.

Almeida, Prakash, *Jinnah Man of Destiny* (Delhi: Kalpaz Publications), 2001.

Ambedkar, B.R., *Pakistan or the Partition of India* (Bombay: Thacker), 1946.

Ambedkar, B.R., *What Congress and Gandhi Have Done to the Untouchables* (Bombay: Thacker & Co.), 1946.

Azad, Maulana Abul Kalam, *India Wins Freedom* (Calcutta: Longmans), 1989.

Azad, Mualana Abul Kalam, *Qual-e-Faizal* (Calcutta: al-Balagh Press), 1922.

Aziz, Beg, *Jinnah and His Time* (Islamabad: Babur and Amer Publications), 1986.

Aziz, K.K., *Rahmat Ali—A Biography* (Lahore: Vanguard), 1987.

Aziz, K. K. *The Making of Pakistan* (London: Chatto & Windus), 1967.

Bakshi, Illahi, *With Quiad-e-Azam During His Last Days* (Karachi: Quaid-e-Azam Academy), 1978.

Baig, M.R.A., *In Different Saddles* (New York: Asia Publications), 1967.

Bamford, P.C., *Histories of Non-Cooperation and Khilafat Movements* (New Delhi: Deep and Deep), 1974.

Bannerjea, D.N., *India's Nation Builder* (London: Headley), 1919.

Beck, Theodore, *Essays on Indian Topics* (Allahabad: Pioneer Press), 1888.

Bhardwaj, K.K., *Pakistan's March to Democracy and Liberalism* (New Delhi: Anmol Publications), 1996.

Bhutani, Surender, *Maulana Azad and Indian Polity* (New Delhi: Shipra Publications), 2006.

Bhutto, Zulfikar Ali, *The Myth of Independence* (London: Oxford University Press), 1969.

Blunt, W.S. *India Under Ripon: A Private Diary* (London: T. Fisher Unwin), 1909.

Bolitho, Hector, *Jinnah: Creator of Pakistan* (London: John Murray), 1954.

Bose, Subhas Chandra, *The Indian Struggle Part II* (Calcutta: Published for Netaji Publishing Society), 1945.

Brass, Paul, *Language, Religion and Politics in Northern India* (Cambridge: Cambridge University Press), 1974.

Brass, Paul R., *The Politics of India Since Independence* (Cambridge: Cambridge University Press), 1994.

Buski, Shahid Javed, *Pakistan, The Continuing Struggle for Nationhood* (Boulder Colo, West View Press), 1991.

Chagla, M.C., *Roses in December: An Autobiography* (Bombay: Bharatiya Vidya Bhawan), 1978.

Chandra, Bipin, *Communalism in India* (New Delhi: Vani Educational Books), 1984.

Chandra, Bipin, *India's Struggle For Independence 1857-1947* (New Delhi: Viking), 1988.

Chandra, Bipin, *Modern India* (New Delhi: NCERT), 1976.

Chandra, Bipin, *Nationalism and Colonialism in Modern India* (New Delhi: Orient Longman's Ltd.), 1979.

Chaudhry, Binayandra Mohan, *Muslim Politics in India* (Calcutta: Orient Longman), 1946.

Chaudhry, Kailash, *Tragedy of Jinnah* (Lahore: Varma Publishing Co.), 1943.

Chaudhri, Munir, *Mir-Mansam* (Dacca: Oxford University Press), 1968.

Chaudhary Rahmat Ali, *Pakistan: The Farther Land of Pak Nation* (London: The Pak National Liberal Movement), 1947.

Chaudhry, Sandhaya, *Gandhi and Partition of India* (New Delhi: Sterling), 1984.

Chiral, Valentine, *India, Old and New* (New Delhi: Light and Life Publishers), 1975.

Chiral, Valentine, *The Indian Unrest* (New Delhi: Light and Life Publishers), 1979.

Chopra, P.N., *Maulana Abul Kalam Azad Unfulfilled Dreams* (New Delhi: Interprint), 1990.

Clifford, Geertz (ed.), *Old Societies and New States: The Quest for Modalities in Asia and Africa* (New York: Free Press), 1963.

Cohen, Stephen Philip, *The Idea of Pakistan* (New Delhi: Oxford University Press), 2005.

Collins Larry and Dominique Lapierre, *Freedom at Midnight* (New Delhi: Vikas Publications), 1973.

Constituent Assembly of Pakistan Debates, 11 August 1947, Vol. I, No. 2, pp. 18-20.

Countess Mary of Minto, *India Minto and Morely 1905-1910* (London: Macmillan), 1934.

Coupland, R., *The Indian Problem Part II* (New York: Oxford University Press), 1944.

Cunning John (ed.), *Political India 1832-1932* (London: Oxford University Press), 1932.

Damodar P. Singhal, *Pakistan* (New Jersey: Prentice Hall), 1972.

Dar, B.A., *Religious Thoughts of Syed Ahmed Khan* (Lahore: Institute of Islamic Culture), 1961.

Das, Durga, *India from Curzon to Nehru and After* (New York: John Doby), 1970.

Datta, S. K. and Rajiv Sharma, *Pakistan from Jinnah to Jehad* (New Delhi: UBSPD), 2002.

De Amalendu, *Roots of Separatism in the Nineteenth Century Bengal* (Calcutta: Maya Prakashan), 1974.

De Amalendu, *Islam in Modern India* (Calcutta: Maya Prakashan), 1982.

Desai, Mahadev, *Maulana Abul Kalam Azad: A Biographical Memoir* (Agra: Shiva Lal Agarwal), 1946.

Dodwell, H.H. (ed.), *The Cambridge History of the British Empire*, Vol. 5 (London: Cambridge University Press), 1932.

Douglas, Ian Henderson, *Abul Kalam Azad: An Intellectual and Religious Biography* (Delhi: Oxford University Press), 1988.

Dutt, R. Palme, *India, Today and Tomorrow* (London: Lawrence and Wishart), 1955.

Dwarkadas, Kanji, *India's Fight for Freedom: An Eye Witness Story, 1913-37* (Bombay: Poplar Prakashan), 1960.

Ernest, Gellner, *"Nationalism" in Thought and Change* (Widenfeld and Nichalson), 1964.

Embree, Ainslie T., *Imaging India: Essays on Indian History* (London: Oxford University Press), 1989.

Escott, T.H.S. (ed.), *The Pillars of the Empire* (London: Chapman & Hall), 1879.

Faruqi, Z.H., *The Deoband School and the Demand for the Pakistan* (Bombay: Asia), 1963

Faruqi, Zakir Hussain, *Muslim League Kiyyum?* (Bombay: Maktaha-Sultani), 1947.

Faruqi, Ziya-ul-Hasan, *Mulana Abul Kalam Azad Towards Freedom* (Delhi: B.R. Publishing Company), 1997

Gaba, K.L., *Inside Pakistan* (Delhi: Raj Kamal Publications), 1948.

Gandhi, M.K., *An Autobiography or The Story of My Experiments With Truth* (Ahmedabad: Navajivan Publishing House), 1983.

Gandhi, M.K., *Hind Swaraj* (Ahmedabad: Navajivan Publishing House), 1982.

Gandhi, Rajmohan, *India Wins Error—A Scrutiny of Maulana Azad's India Wins Freedom* (New Delhi: Penguin), 2002.

Gerth, H.H. and C. Wright Mills (eds.), *From Max Weber Essays in Sociology* (London: Routledge), 1991.

Gopal, S., *Selected Works of Jawaharlal Nehru*, Vol. I (New Delhi: Orient Longman), 1972.

Graham, G.F.I., *The Life and Work of Sir Syed Ahmed Khan* (London: Oxford University Press), 1974.

Gunther, John, *Inside Asia* (New York: Hamilton), 1938.

Hali, Altaf Hussain, *Hayat-i-Jawed* (Delhi; Idarah-i-Adabiyat-i-Delhi), 1979.

Hameed, Syeda Saiyidain, *Islamic Seal on India: Independence, Abul Kalam Azad – A Fresh Look* (Karachi: Oxford), 1998.

Hamid, Abdul, *Muslim Separatism in India* (Lahore: OUP), 1967.

Hamid, Shahid, *Disastrous Twilight* (Leo-Cooper: Oxford University Press), 1986.

Haq, Mushir-ul, *Muslim Politics in Modern India* (Meerut: Meenakshi Prakashan), 1970.

Hasan, Mushir-ul (ed.), *Islam and Indian Nationalism: Reflections on Abul Kalam Azad* (Delhi: Manohar), 1992.

Hassan, Javed, *India: A Study in Profile* (Rawalpindi: Army Book Service), 1990.

Hasan, S.S., *Plain Mr. Jinnah: Selections from Quaid-e-Azam correspondence relating mainly to personal matters* (Karachi: Royal Book Company), 1976.

Hedayatullah, Mohammad, *Sayyid Ahmad Khan: A Study of the Religious Reform of Movement of Sayyid Ahmad Khan of Rae Bareli* (Lahore: Ashraf), 1970.

Hudson, H.V., *The Great Divide* (Karachi: Oxford University Press), 1969.

Hussain, S. Abid (ed.), *The Destiny of Indian Muslims* (Bombay: Asia), 1965.

Hussain, Azim, *Fazl-i-Husain* (Bombay: Longmans), 1946.

Iqbal Afzal (ed.), *Select Writings and Speeches of Maulana Mohamed Ali* (Lahore: Ashsaf), 1944.

Ikram, S.M., *Modern Muslim India and the Birth of Pakistan* (Lahore: S.M. Ikram), 1965.

Jain, M.S., *The Aligarh Movement: Its Origin and Development 1858-1906* (Agra: Sri Ram Mehra), 1965.

Jalal, Ayesha, *The Sole Spokesman: Jinnah, The Muslim League and The Demand for Pakistan* (Cambridge: Cambridge University Press), 1985.

Jayakar, M.R., *The Story of My Life, Vol. II* (Bombay: Asia Publishing House), 1959.

Jawed, Ajeet, *Secular and Nationalist Jinnah* (New Delhi: Kitab Publishing House), 1998.

Jinnah, Fatima, *My Brother* (Karachi: Qaid-e-Azam Academy), 1987.

Jinnah, M.A., *History of the Origin of Fourteen Points* (Bombay: n.d), mf (Australia: Flinders University).

Joachim, Alva, *Leaders of India* (Bombay: Thacker and Company), 1943.

Kabir, Humayun, *Mulana Abul Kalam Azad: A Memorial Volume* (Bombay: Asia), 1959.

Kanji, Dwarkadas, *Ten Years to Freedom* (Bombay: Popular Prakashan), 1968.

Karunakaran, *Indian Political Thought 1832-1921* (New Delhi: Peacock), 1976.

Kashysp, Subhash C. (ed.), *Maulana Abul Kalam Azad: A Centenary Volume* (New Delhi: National), 1989

Khaliquzzaman, Chaudhri, *Pathway to Pakistan* (Lahore: Pakistan Longman), 1961.

Khan, Sir Syed Ahmed, *Asbab-i-Baghavat-i-Hind* (Agra: Matba-i-Mufidi), 1859.

Khan, Sir Syed Ahmed, *Khutbat-i-Ahmadiya* (Aligarh: Institute Press), 1983.

Khan, Sir Syed Ahmed, *Sirat-i-Faridiyah* (Agra: Matba-i-Mufidi), 1886 (Translation by Chr. Schackle).

Khan, Sir Syed Ahmed, *al-Tahrir fi usul al-tafsir* (Agra: Mufid-i-am Press), 1892.

Khan, Sir Syed Ahmed, *Tusanif-i-Ahmadiyah* (Aligarh: Institute Press), 1883.

Khan, Wali, *Facts are Facts – The Untold Story of Partisan* (New Delhi: Vikas Publications), 1987.

Khurshid, K.H., *Memories of Jinnah* (Karachi: Oxford University Press), 1990.

Kripalani, J.B., *Gandhi: His Life and Thought* (New Delhi: Publications Division, Ministry of Information and Broadcasting, Government of India), 1970.

Lal Bahadur, *The Muslim League, Its History, Activities and Achievements* (Agra: Agra Book Stores), 1954, p. 23.

Lentizion, Nehemia (ed.), *Conversion to Islam* (New York: Holmes and Meir), 1979.

Letters of Iqbal to Jinnah, published by Muhammad Ashraf quoted in Rafiq Zakaria, *The Man Who Divided Pakistan* (Mumbai: Popular Prakashan), 2002.

Lohia, Ram Manohar, *Guilty Men of India's Partition* (Allahabad: Kitabistan), 1960.

Malihabadi, Abdur Razzaq, *Azad Ki Kahani Khud Azad Ki Zubani* (Calcutta: Daftar Azad Hind), 1960.

Malihabadi, Abdur Razzaq, *Zikar-e-Azad* (Calcutta: Daftar Azad Hind), 1960.

Malik, Hafeez, *Muslim Nationalism in India and Pakistan* (Washington D.C: Public Affairs Press), 1963.

Malik, Hafeez (ed.), *Pakistan Founders' Aspirations and To-days Realities* (New York: Oxford University Press), 2001.

Malik, Ram (ed.), *Ghubar-e-Khatir* (New Delhi: Sahitya Academi), 1967.

Malsaini Arsh, *Abul Kalam Azad* (New Delhi: Publications Division, Ministry of Information and Broadcasting, Government of India), 1976.

Mansergh, Nicholas, E.W.R. *Lumby and Penderel Moon, The Transfer of Power 1942-47* (London: Her Majesty Stationery Office), 1970-83.

Masani, R.P., *Dadabhai Naoroji* (New Delhi: Publications Division, Ministry of Information and Broadcasting, Government of India), 1960.

Mazumdar, A.K., *Advent of Independence* (Bombay: Bharatiya Vidya Bhawan), 1963.

Majumdar, B.B., *Indian Political Association and Reforms of Legislatures (1818-1917)* (Calcutta: Minerva), 1945.

Mazumdar, R.C.; Rayachaudhary, H.C. & Dutta, Kali Kumar, *An Advanced History of India* (Madras: Macmillan), 1963.

McGrath, Allen, *The Destruction of Democracy in Pakistan* (Karachi: Oxford University Press), 1972.

Mehrotra, S.R., *Towards India Freedom and Partition* (Delhi: Rupa), 1979.

Menon, V.P., *Transfer of Power*, Vol. VIII (New Delhi: Orient Longman), 1968.

Merriam, Allen Hayes, *Gandhi Vs Jinnah: The Debate Over the Pakistan of India* (Calcutta: Minerva), 1980.

Mirza, Humanyun, *From Plassey to Pakistan* (New York: University Press of America), 1999.

Mody, Hormi, *Pherozeshah Mehta* (New Delhi: Publications Division, Ministry of Information and Broadcasting, Government of India), 1963.

Mohan, Sulakshana, *Pakistan Under Musharraf* (New Delhi: Indian Publishers), 1999.

Moon, Penderel, *Divide and Quit* (London: Chatto & Windus), 1964.

Moore, R.J., *Churchill, Cripps and India 1939-45* (Oxford: Oxford University Press), 1975.

Morley, John Viscount, *Recollections*, Vol. II (London: Macmillan), 1918.

Morrison, Theodore, *The History of the Mohammedan Oriental College, Aligarh, from its Foundation to the Year 1903* (Aligarh: Institute Press), 1904.

Mujeeb, M., *The Indian Muslims* (London: Allen and Unwin), 1967.

Mustafa, Zubeida (ed.), *The South Asian Century: 1900-1999* (London: Oxford University Press), 2000.

Naidu, Sarojini (ed.), *Mohammad Ali Jinnah, An Ambassador of Unity: His Speeches and Writings* (Madras: Ganesh), 1918.

Nanda, B.R., *Gandhi, Pan-Islamism, Imperialism and Nationalism in India* (Bombay: Oxford University Press), 1989.

Nehru, Jawaharlal, *An Autobiography* (London: The Bodley Head), 1937.

Page, D., *Prelude to Pakistan* (Delhi: Oxford University Press), 1982.

Panipati, M. Ismail, *Maqalat-i-Sir Sayyid* (Lahore: Majlis-i-taraqqi-i-adab), 1972.

Prashad, Rajendra, *India Divided* (Bombay: Hinkd Kitabs), 1947.

Pirzada, Syed Sharifuddin, *Quaid-e-Azam Jinnah's Correspondence* (New Delhi: Metropolitan Book Company), 1981.

Pirzada, S.S. (ed.), *Foundations of Pakistan, All India Muslim League Documents 1906-1947* (New Delhi: Metropolitan Book Company), 1982.

Pirzada, Syed Sharifuddin, *Some Aspects of Qaid-e-Azam's Life* (Islamabad: National Commission on Historical and Cultural Research), 1978.

Pirzada, S.S. (ed.), *The Collected Works of Quaid-e-Azam Mohammad Ali Jinnah*, Vol. I (Karachi: East West Publishing), 1969.

Radhakrishnan, S. (ed.), *Mahatma Gandhi* (London: George Allen), 1949.

Ralhan, O. P. (ed.), *Hindu Mahasabha*, Vol. II (New Delhi: Anmol), 1997.

Ramani, Hashoo Kewal, *Pakistan X-Rayed* (Delhi: New Age Publication), 1955.

Ram Gopal, Indian Muslim (Bombay: Asia Publishing House), 1959.

Rawlinson, H.G., *The British Achievements in India* (London: William Hodge), 1948.

Resolutions of the All India Muslim League from March 1941 to April 1942 (Delhi: All India Muslim League).

Robinson, F., *Separation Among Muslims* (Cambridge: Cambridge University Press), 1974.

Roy, M.N., *Men I Met* (New Delhi: Lalvani Publications), 1968.

Sahni, J.N., *The Lid Off* (Bombay: Allied Publishers), 1971.

Sarojini, *Speeches and Writings* (Madras: G.A. Natesan), 1945.

Sayed, Khalid B., *Pakistan: The Formation Phase 1857-1948* (London: Oxford University Press), 1968.

Sayed, Zaifullah and Samuel Baid, *Pakistan: An End Without a Beginning* (Delhi: Lancer International).

Saiyidain, K.G., *Maluana Azad's Contribution to Education* (Baroda: The Maharaja Sayajirao University), 1961.

Sayid, M.H., The Sound of Fury: A Political Study of Mohammad Ali Jinnah (New Delhi: Akbar Publishing House), 1983.

Spear, Percival, India Pakistan and the West (London: Oxford University Press), 1958.

Sitaramayya, B. Pattabhi, *The History of Indian National Congress*, Vol. I, 1985-1935 (Bombay: Padma Publications), 1946.

Seervai, H.M., *Partition of India – Legend and Reality* (Bombay: Emmenem Publishers), 1989.

Sharma, Jai Narain, "Irreligious Jinnah Wanted A Religious Pak", *The Tribune*, Chandigarh, 6 July 1997.

Sharma, Jai Narain, *Power, Politics and Corruption: A Gandhian Solution* (New Delhi: Deep and Deep), 2004.

Sharma, M.S.M., *Peeps Into Pakistan* (Patna: Pustak Bhandar), 1954.

Sharma, Rashmi (ed.), *Sonia Versus Vajpayee* (New Delhi: Deep and Deep), 2004.

Sharma, T.L., *Hindu Muslim Relations, 1913-1925* (Delhi: B. R. Publishing Corporation), 1987.

Sharif, *Al-Mujahid Qaide-e-Azam* (Delhi: Low Price Publications), 1993.

Sherwani, Latif Ahmad, *Pakistan Resolution to Pakistan* (Delhi: Daya Publishing House), 1985.

Sikander Hayat, *Pakistan Resolution Revisited* (Islamabad: National Institute of Historical and Cultural Research), 1999.

Singh, Anita Inder, *The Origin of the Partition of India 1936-47* (Bombay: Oxford University Press), 1987.

Singh, Mahavir (ed.), *Mulana Abul Kalam Azad: Profile of a Nationalist* (New Delhi Anamika), 2003.

Sitaramayya, Pattabhi, History of Indian National Congress (Delhi: S. Chand & Co.), 1969.

Smith, W.C., Modern Islam in India (London: V. Golanez), 1946.

Sri Prakash, *Pakistan: Birth and Early Days* (New Delhi: Meenakshi Prakashan), 1965.

Suda, J.P., *Main Currents of Social and Political Thought in India*, Vol. III (Meerut: K. Nath & Co.), 1973.

Symonds, Richard, *Making of Pakistan* (London: Faber and Faber), 1950.

Tara Chand, *History of Freedom Movement in India* (New Delhi: Publications Division, Ministry of Information and Broadcasting, Government of India), 1962.

Tendulkar, D.G., *Mahatma*, 8 Vols. (New Delhi: Publications Division, Ministry of Information and Broadcasting, Government of India), 1958.

The Collected Works of Mahatma Gandhi (New Delhi: Publications Division, Ministry of Information and Broadcasting, Government of India), 1966.

Troll, Christian W., *Sayyid Ahmad Khan: A Reinterpretation of Muslim Theology* (New Delhi: Vikas), 1978.

Varma, V.P., *Modern Indian Political Thought* (Agra: Luxmi Narain Agarwal), 1961.

Wells, Ian Bryant, *Jinnah's Early Politics: Ambassador of Hindu Muslim Unity* (Delhi: Permanent Black), 2005.

Wolpert, Stanley, *Jinnah of Pakistan* (New York: Oxford University Press), 1984.

Wolpert, S., *Tilak and Gokhale: Revolution and Reform in the Making of Modern India* (Barkeley: University of California Press), 1961.

Zaidi, A.M. and Shaheda Zaidi (eds.), *The Encyclopedia of Indian National Congress*, Vol. IV, 1901-1905 (New Delhi: S. Chand & Co.), 1978.

Zakaria, Rafiq, *The Man Who Divided India* (Mumbai: Popular Prakashan), 2002.

Zakaria, Rafiq, *Price of Partition* (Mumbai: Bharatiya Vidaya Bhawan), 1998.

Zulfikar, G. H., *Pakistan: As Visualised by Iqbal and Jinnah* (Lahore: Bajm-e-Iqbal), 1989.

Index